IRISH CARVED ORNAMENT

A DESIGN OF EIGHT HUMAN FIGURES INTERLACED.

FROM MUIREDACH'S CROSS, MONASTERBOICE.

See also Plate XXXV.

IRISH CARVED ORNAMENT

from Monuments of the Christian Period

Henry S. Crawford, B.A., B.A.I., M.R.I.A., F.R.S.A.I.

with a preface for this edition
by
Michael Herity, M.A., Ph.D., F.S.A.

The design at A, Fig 12, adapted to a circular panel

Published in collaboration with
The Royal Society of Antiquaries of Ireland
by

THE MERCIER PRESS

Mercier Press
www.mercierpress.ie

First published 1927 by The Royal Society of Antiquaries of Ireland.

This edition published by Mercier Press in 1980.

© Mercier Press 1980

ISBN 978 1 78117 859 1

Transferred to digital print on demand in 2023.

Acknowledgements

The Commissioners of Public Works, Ireland: Plates 1–11, XIVA and LI
Historic Monuments and Building Branch, Department of the Environment for Northern Ireland: VI (Arboe).

A CIP record for this title is available from the British Library.

PREFACE

UNDERTAKING, at the request of my friend, Mr. Crawford, the pleasant duty of writing a preface to his work on *Irish Carved Ornament*, I cannot but feel conscious of a sense of superfluity. Surely a book such as this needs no commendation: surely it is itself a better eulogy of its author, and of the Society which has undertaken its publication, than anything that I could pen!

I can testify from personal knowledge that the size of the book is no indication of the great labour that has made it possible—a labour extending over many years. Mr. Crawford has personally visited most, if not all, of the monuments upon which he draws for his materials; as well as many more, which he has not found occasion to mention, although a knowledge of them was lying in the background of his mind while he was preparing his work. He has devoted to his task, of illustrating one side of the art of our ancient forerunners, a very considerable skill in photography and in draughtsmanship. The pious old Irish chroniclers used to dedicate their labours: To the Glory of God, and the Honour of the Saints of the Land of Ireland. Mr. Crawford may well claim to have worked in the same reverent spirit, with the important addition, that he has also made a valuable contribution to the modern scientific study of ancient art.

We are only beginning to realise the complexity of the problem of the origins, affinities, and history of what is commonly called " Celtic " art. Salin, Reginald A. Smith, Baldwin Brown, Strzygowski, Baron de Baye, and a host of others have been for years engaged in collecting materials on the subject, and on the closely related Teutonic art of the same period, which must be taken into consideration by anyone who wishes to make any real study of the Celtic monuments. Bröndsted, in his recently published work on *Early English Ornament*, has isolated a phase of Anglian art which he traces directly to a Syrian source; which, indeed, can hardly have been imported into England at all, except by specially introduced Syrian sculptors. The influence of these Oriental craftsmen spread far beyond the district where they worked; we can trace it even on the Muiredach Cross at Monasterboice. But to grapple with all the problems to which recent researches have given rise, and to reduce the principles of Teutonic and Celtic art to some systematic order, will be a work for several generations of scholars.

Mr. Crawford's book is an addition of no small importance to the materials available for study. The richness of Irish ornament in MS. Illumination was a familiar commonplace; but no one who had not actually examined the monuments themselves, with the same assiduity as Mr. Crawford, could have formed any idea of the wealth of this country in the analogous sculptured art. The few literary sources of information are inadequate, and for the greater part are out of print and with difficulty accessible. The best of them—the collection of drawings published by the late Henry O'Neill—gives a very good idea of the appearance of each cross as a whole, but for purposes of analysis it is quite insufficient; and without analysis of the ornament, panel by panel, no true idea of its wealth and variety, or of its history and development can be obtained.

The study of iconography will also benefit by Mr. Crawford's collection. We do not appear to have any scenes from Pre-Christian sagas sculptured on the Irish crosses, such as add an immense interest to those of the Isle of Man. In fact, most of the scenes are directly derived from the Biblical history. There are however a few problematical figure panels, on which the last word has by no means yet been said. In this connection I may mention an ingenious suggestion made to me by Prof. T. Ó Máille, of Galway, to the effect that the strange procession with a headless horseman, shown on the base of the Ahenny Cross and on the head of the cross at Dromiskin, is a record of the catastrophe which took place in Ireland about the time when those crosses must have been made—the death in battle and the decapitation of Cormac mac Cuillenáin, the famous king and archbishop of Cashel. · (See No. 150.)

Mr. Crawford has set before us a goodly feast. We partake, we are grateful; but we are not satisfied; we follow the example of Oliver Twist, and ask for more! The sculptured stones of Scotland are all collected together for the world's instruction, in a huge volume with hundreds of photographic and other illustrations. When will some wealthy patron arise, who will realise that politics are not the only possible outlet for patriotism, and who will subsidise the preparation of a similar volume for Ireland? When such a benefactor makes his appearance, the man to carry out the work is clearly marked out in the author of the book now in the reader's hands.

R. A. S. MACALISTER.

PREFACE

to the second edition

Henry Saxton Crawford was born at Celbridge, the son of a gentleman farmer. Educated at the High School, he entered Trinity College Dublin in October 1886 at the age of nineteen, graduating BA, BAI in 1891. In 1904 he was elected a member of our Society and made his first contribution to volume *36* of the *Journal* in January 1906 with the description of **an** ogham stone at Ballingarry, Co. Limerick. He wrote three further contributions, all illustrated with good photographs, for the same volume and from then on to volume *57* every volume of the *Journal* had one or several pieces by him, often illustrated with his signed drawings or with his photographs, the writing always clear and concise.

Most of the material described by him is from the early Christian and later medieval periods, but his work also includes the description of a quern, its fittings and the method of dressing it with a *breacaire* (*39*, 393), accounts of the castles at Loughmoe and Carrick-on-Suir, Co. Tipperary (*39*, 243, 255), the identification of a chi-rho symbol at Glendalough (*42*, 60), a short account of St Brigid's Crosses of straw from Clare and south Roscommon (*38*, 394; *39*, 399) and the discovery of Graves's drawings of the La Tène bone slips from the Lough Crew tombs, the originals of which were at that time lost (*44*, 161). He also wrote the first thorough description of the Romanesque doorway at Clonfert (*42*, 1), as well as descriptions of three bell-shrines in museums in London, the Bearnán Cuilean, St Mura's and St Conall's (*52*, 1).

His two great contributions to the *Journal* are the papers on Crosses and Cross-Slabs in volumes *37*, *42* and *43*. The first of these is a list in 52 pages of all free-standing crosses, the rude and small as well as the ornate, which are listed by County, Townland and Six-Inch Sheet, with a note, where relevant, of the nearest railway station. The list was drawn up 'for convenience in the preparation of a series of photographs of the crosses' and was the first national survey of field monuments since Borlase's *Dolmens of Ireland* (1897). The listing of the railway station implies that members would travel by rail and possibly on by bicycle to inspect the sites. Crawford realised the importance of this kind of listing and modestly suggested that 'lists of the several classes of ancient monuments existing in the country' might one day be prepared.

In volumes *42* and *43* he listed slabs, giving the same details about location and adding a short descriptive note in each case. In the very brief intro-duction, he put forward in his concise style a typological development from simple to complex and the now familiar idea that free-standing crosses derived from slabs with slight projections on either side (*42*, 218).

Crawford is listed as a member of the Society's Council for the years 1909-11, as a Vice-President for Munster in 1924 and as joint Hon. Librarian in the same year. In 1926 the present work appeared with a Preface by his friend, Professor R. A. S. Macalister. Macalister noted that the preparation of the book was 'a labour extending over many years', observing that the best collection of descriptions of the crosses previously available was the nineteenth-century compilation of Henry O'Neill and pointing out that a similar work on the sculptured slabs, like the great Allen-Anderson catalogue for Scotland, published in 1903, should be begun.

Unfortunately, Crawford died in March 1927 at the age of sixty shortly after the appearance of this book, which is now, happily, being reprinted. It is today as useful as ever as a comprehensive corpus and analysis of these carvings, a monument to comparative archaeology. In this age of near-perfection in lens design, in camera miniaturisation and in colour photography, it is salutary to read the patient words of advice in Crawford's *Introduction* about creating the right natural lighting conditions for the crosses. Happily his vast collection of negatives is housed in the National Museum.

Michael Herity

Contents

List of Figures in Text

Tailpieces, etc.

List of Plates

CARVED ORNAMENT FROM IRISH MONUMENTS

CHAPTER I.

INTRODUCTION

everal books have of late years become available for the study of Celtic design as applied to
manuscripts, and in them, no doubt, the art found its
highest, or at least its most complex, development. But
objects of metal and stone were frequently decorated
in the same style, and in comparison have been
neglected so far as Irish examples are concerned.

As regards metal work, the admirable plates and
descriptions in Mr. Coffey's *Guide to the Celtic Antiquities of the Christian
Period, in the National Museum*, give much valuable information; though
one could wish to have larger photographs and more extended descriptions
of these as well as other objects of the kind.

The character of ornamental design necessarily varies with the
material employed; on stone the designs are generally bold and simple,
and may be usefully studied as an introduction to, or in connection with
those drawn on parchment. In addition to the absence of great
complexity, carved work offers, owing to the large scale on which it is
executed, the advantage of being easily examined. On the other hand
it has the inconvenience that the examples available for study are
scattered through the country, and that many of them have become
indistinct owing to centuries of weather wear and to the disfiguring growth
of lichen.

The purpose of this book is to illustrate the various types of design
found on Irish monuments of the ninth, tenth, and eleventh centuries,
and to remedy as far as possible the disadvantages mentioned above, by
bringing together a classified series of examples and by showing them
restored as well as in their present condition. The variety of the designs
is so great, and there is so little exact repetition, that difficulty arises as

to the number to be included. This number has been repeatedly extended, and still those given might with advantage be supplemented by others, especially in the classes of Zoömorphic ornament and pictorial scenes.

Drawings of some of the panels illustrated have already been published, but no attention has been paid to this, as it is of less importance to show new patterns than to gather together a typical series of the best preserved specimens, and to arrange them in a form admitting of ready comparison. The writings of the late Mr. J. Romilly Allen on Celtic art and the sculptured monuments of Scotland must here be referred to, as he has so clearly set out the principles and methods of constructing Celtic patterns, and has published so many illustrations of Scottish carving, that little need be said on these points. This series of designs from Irish monuments should, however, be of interest, if only for comparison with the Scottish ones, and as a record of carved work which is gradually disappearing.

Photographs are the most accurate and satisfactory form of illustration, but few who have not tried this branch of the art realise the difficulty of producing the best results. Carvings of early date are generally so worn by the weather, and have lost so much sharpness that they will not show at all clearly unless the light is just right both in quality and direction. It should be at the same time bright and diffused, and should make with the plane of the surface, an angle more or less acute according to the depth of the cutting and the roughness of the stone.

Carved panels, therefore, should be photographed at various hours of the day so as to suit the directions in which they face. Those looking north are never properly illuminated except in the early mornings or late evenings of the months of June and July; and as many of the monuments are in remote places, it is difficult to be on the ground at those hours. Even if the conditions described are fulfilled, lichens and stains may prevent success; *the light and shade due to the relief being confused with that caused by the varying colour.* Anything high above the ground requires a scaffold or platform; and the situation of some designs is such as to render a good photograph hardly possible—on the upper and under sides of cross-arms and rings for instance—or it may be that there is a wall or other obstruction in front. Other carvings are placed in dark buildings or under trees which cast unequal shadows.

To photograph well a carved surface should be approximately of one colour, and, therefore, though odd panels can be satisfactorily taken direct, the only way to obtain a uniform series of illustrations is to work from *casts.* They have the necessary evenly coloured surface and can be placed in a suitable light. Such casts as were already available have been made use of, and in many other cases casts have been specially made. In this connection thanks are due to the authorities of the National Museum for allowing their casts to be used, and otherwise assisting. For the remainder it has been necessary to trust to the best photographs obtainable from the stone in spite of stains and other difficulties, including limited time.

Plates XV. to L. are chiefly devoted to designs in rectangular and other panels. and two photographs of each are given, one plain and the other restored as far as may be, thus showing the present state of the carving, and its original appearance as inferred from a careful study. Panels in good preservation have been chosen, whenever possible, in order to avoid doubtful points in the restoration; any such are mentioned in the descriptions, or may be seen by comparison with the untouched photographs. It should be remembered, however, that the original stones and also rubbings have been examined, and information sometimes obtained from them which hardly appears in the photographs.

Designs in the same style as those shown in the plates are freely used to decorate borders and circular centrepieces; a number of these are given as diagrams in the text. With the circular designs are included some of the semicircular and other patterns used to fill the extremities of incised crosses at Clonmacnois and elsewhere. The original carvings vary so much in size that it has been found necessary to reduce them to similar dimensions; they are accordingly not to scale, but the size of each is given: the measurements being in the case of the drawings, the greatest length and breadth of the part shown, and in the plates those of the panels *inside* the surrounding borders.

In a work of this kind the illustrations should be the principal feature, the letterpress being, for the most part, explanatory of them. The arrangement, therefore, is such as to facilitate reference from each figure to its description, and *vice versa*. The photographs in Plates XV. to L. are numbered consecutively and are throughout referred to as *Number so and so*. The drawings are separately numbered and always alluded to as *Figure so and so*. An index of the forty-eight localities from which designs have been taken is given at the end, together with the reference numbers of the illustrations from each.

A PANEL FROM DRUMCLIFF CROSS.

Showing Frets, Spirals and Knots united in one Design.

CHAPTER II.

CLASSES OF MONUMENTS AND DESIGNS

ALL the designs illustrated in Plates XV. to L. and Figures 1 to 12 are taken from crosses, sepulchral slabs, and pillar stones.

The High Crosses are the chief storehouses of early carved ornament, and have furnished the greater number of the abstract designs and almost all those consisting of human and animal forms. The finest of these crosses have a great resemblance to each other, and were erected early in the tenth century.

Their chief characteristics are the square slightly tapering base and shaft, the latter divided into panels occupied by separate designs: the encircling ring, the large rounded hollows at the intersection, and the shrine or house-shaped top. The hollows usually contain " rolls " passing from front to back, and attached either to the ring or to the cross itself.

Typical examples of High Crosses are given in Plates I. to VIII. The Ahenny monuments, Plates I. and II., are evidently the earliest in date; they, with several others of the same type,[1] show that the scale of proportions afterwards used had not then been fixed or the shrine-shaped cap evolved. Another early feature is the free use and high quality of the spiral patterns, and the way in which they differ from those on other crosses. None of the spiral coils, for instance, are raised to form bosses in relief. Most important of all is the similarity of the ornament to that seen in the illuminated manuscripts of the eighth century.

For these reasons the Ahenny crosses may be assigned to the middle of the ninth century, a date which follows and agrees with the appearance of the ringed cross on sepulchral slabs. Plate I. shows the west face of the North Cross; this monument is 12 ft. 6 in. in height, and is edged with rope moulding partly broken away, it is said purposely to make scythe stones. The head is covered with trumpet pattern, undoubtedly the finest example in the country of that motive as applied

---

[1] Two crosses at Kilkieran, County Kilkenny, and two broken shafts at Lorrha, in North Tipperary.

to stone (Plate XIVA). The other side of the head is decorated with interlaced work (Plate LI.), and on each face of the shaft there are two panels arranged to contrast with each other. The base is partially buried, but the scenes carved on it are illustrated separately—Nos. 126, 148, 150, 155.

Plate II. illustrates the west and south sides of the South Cross, 11 ft. in height. It is in more perfect condition than the North Cross, except as to the base which is much worn. One of the eight hunting scenes from the base is shown in No. 153, the others are very indistinct. Both faces of the head are in this case covered with a continuous pattern of broken plait, composed of double bands. The shaft is carved all over with spiral or trumpet pattern. Slightly later in date is the cross at Bealin, near Athlone; from it several panels are illustrated, especially No. 91; a striking design also found in illuminated manuscripts.

The Cross at Durrow Abbey, Plate III., is a good example of the crosses erected in the tenth century; it is about 13 ft. in height. Crosses of this kind form the most numerous class of decorated monuments, and exhibit the increasing use of the human figure as shown in actual scenes: geometrical designs, when used, are simpler and on a larger scale; spirals having a tendency to disappear. The plate gives the east side on which can be recognised *The Last Judgment* and *The Sacrifice of Isaac*.[2]

Plate IV. contains front and side views of the Cross of Muiredach at Monasterboice, the finest of these monuments; from it have been taken many of the designs given in this book. It has often been illustrated, usually by perspective views, but these elevations seem to give a clearer idea of its proportions and symmetry. Its height is 17 ft. 8 in.; both figures and geometrical designs appear in its decoration.[3] On the west side, shown in the plate, is seen a characteristic example of the Crucifixion as represented in Celtic Art. The frontispiece is a panel from the south side of this cross representing eight human figures interlaced in the manner often seen in Irish illuminated manuscripts. This design is also shown on a small scale with the other carvings; it is No. 95, Plates XXXV. and XXXVI.

Figure 1 is a drawing by the late T. J. Westropp, of the principal cross at Clonmacnois. This monument is of special interest, as it is several times mentioned in the ancient annals under the names of " The High Cross " and " The Cross of the Scriptures." It is 12½ ft. in height, and bears two mutilated inscriptions in which can be traced the names of King Flann and Abbot Colman.[4] The date is thus fixed to the first quarter of the tenth century; practically it is the same as that of the Cross of Muiredach, to which it corresponds in many ways. Each has on the shaft a panel of eight men interlaced; each has the Divine Hand carved on the under side of one arm and has twists of serpents encircling human heads, on the lower surface of the ring. This cross has, however,

[2] Miss M. Stokes, *High Crosses of Castledermot and Durrow.*
[3] Dr. R. A. S. Macalister, *Muiredach, his Life and Surroundings.* The cross was erected, according to the inscription, before the year 924.
[4] T. J. Westropp, *Journal, Royal Soc. Antiquaries, Ireland,* vol. xxxvii (1907), p. 290.

several features peculiar to itself, such as the tapering shape and slight upward tilt of the arms; also the complete ring shown as passing in front of the shaft and arms instead of disappearing into them, as in the other crosses illustrated. Panels from this cross are shown in Nos. 105, 143, 146, 157, 160.

In Plate V. is seen the South Cross at Castledermot, Co. Kildare: 12 ft. in height. This cross is of granite and has a simpler outline than those formed of sandstone; there is, for instance, no separate cap. The east side is decorated by panels of geometrical ornament, several of which are reproduced in the plates: the other sides bear figures and scenes, several taken from the Scriptures.[5] There is a seated harper on one arm, and figures, which probably represent the Apostles, on the shaft. The base is partially carved; the west has two men driving a number of animals, and the south shows the Miracle of the Loaves and Fishes.

Plate VI. contains elevations of two tall, slender crosses. The first of these, situated on the shore of Lough Neagh at Arboe Point, in Co. Tyrone, is about 19 ft. in height; it closely follows the standard type and is the second tallest of the Irish crosses. The decoration chiefly consists of panels with figure subjects in high relief, amongst them can be recognised—The Fall of Man, The Sacrifice of Isaac, The Man between rampant animals, The Children in the Furnace, The Last Judgment, The Flight into Egypt and the Crucifixion.[6]

The second cross in this plate is that of Moone Abbey, Co. Kildare; this is a granite cross, 17 ft. 6 in. in height, and formed of three stones. The base is higher and narrower than usual and has three carved panels on each side; the upper part of the monument displays a number of animal patterns and a crucifixion so conventionalised that it looks like a Greek cross provided with head, hands and feet. A crucifixion of the ordinary type occupies one of the panels on the base. Miss M. Stokes has fully described this cross.[7]

Plate VII. illustrates the Cross of Drumcliff near Sligo; 12 ft. 7 in. in height. In it the head is reduced in size; some of the figures are in very high relief as compared with others, and the designs are framed in rows of pellets instead of plain beads or ropework. These changes indicate a slightly later period, probably the end of the tenth century.[8] It is remarkable that a small opening has been pierced through behind one of the angle beads of the shaft; this may be due to some recollection of the earlier use of *Holed Stones*. Several other crosses have perforations through the centre of the head.

In Plate VIII. are shown front and side views of a late eleventh century cross; that of Dysert O'Dea, Co. Clare, 11 ft. 6 in. in height, in which many differences are at once apparent. The ring has disappeared, and the human figures are large and in high relief: spirals and plain interlacing

---

[5] Same reference as note 2.

[6] F. J. Bigger and W. J. Fennell, *Ulster Journal of Archaeology*, vol. iv. (1897), p. 1. Some of the identifications of subjects given in this paper cannot, however, be regarded as correct.

[7] *Transactions, R. I. Academy*, vol. xxxi. (1900), p. 541.

[8] Same reference as note 7.

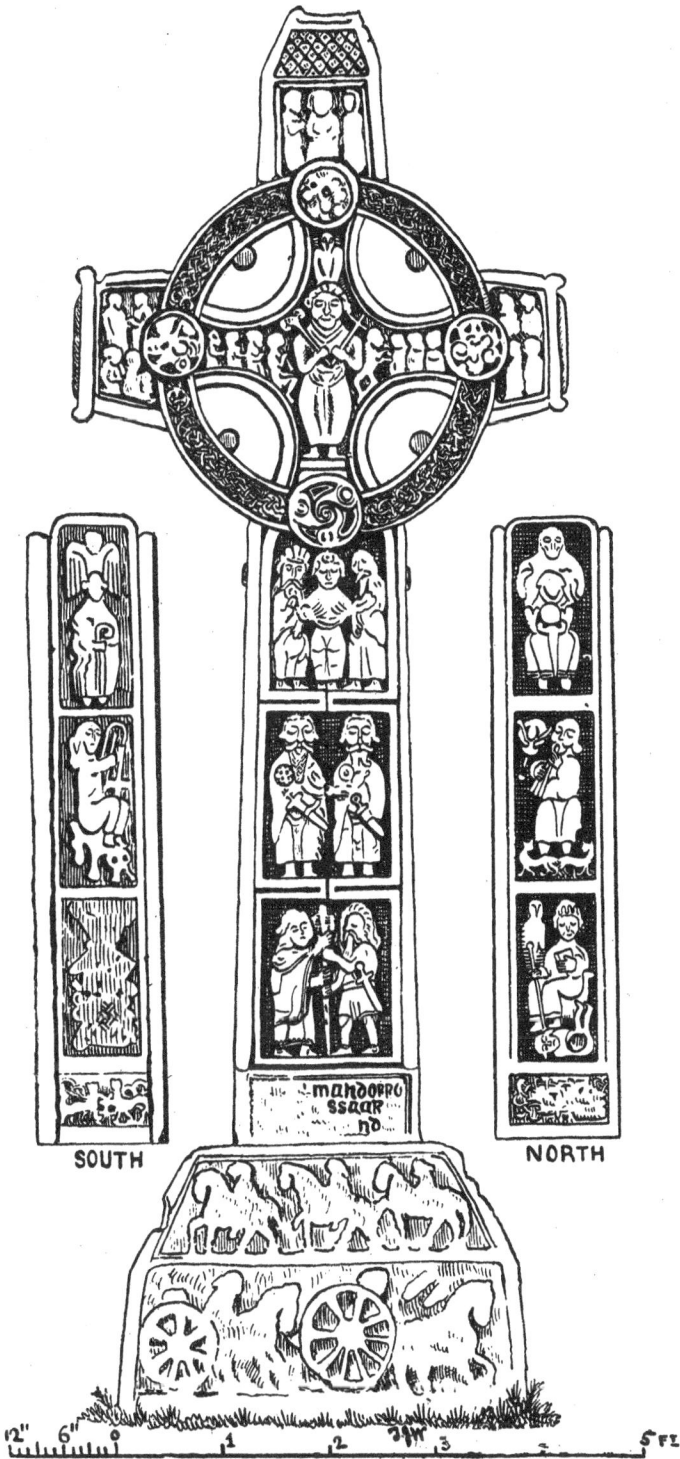

Fig. 1.—The Cross of the Scriptures, Clonmacnois.
(The East Face, &c., drawn by the late T. J. Westropp.)

SOUTH

NORTH

have almost ceased to be carved, and the panels are filled with fret patterns and Zoömorphic designs; the latter deeply cut and having the animals represented in full vigour; there are also traces of leaf-work.[9]   Another cross of this kind, but later in date, is preserved in St. Kevin's Oratory at Glendalough.

The ornament of the twelfth century shows further deterioration; of this the Tuam cross is a striking example.   The panels are almost all filled with Zoömorphic patterns which have lost their strength; the relief is slight and the animals are conventionalised to such an extent as to suggest a new style of geometrical interlaced ornament.   Patterns of the same kind are worked on the processional Cross of Cong, and on the Shrine of St. Lactan's Arm.

In Ireland there are but few of the large erect slabs which are so numerous in Scotland.   Several are, however, shown in Plates IX., X., XI., XII.   Plate IX. from Fahan Mura, Co. Donegal, is a slab 7 ft. in height, on each side of which is carved in relief a handsome interlaced cross.   The opposite side is seen in No. 55, Plates XXV. and XXVI.

Plate X. shows the pillar or slab which stands in the churchyard at Carndonagh, Co. Donegal.   This has on the west side a star of seven points on a fretwork stem between two human figures, and below a star or cross pattern of four points.   On the east side is a rude crucifixion and an interlaced cross with a fretwork base.

In Plate XI. is illustrated a more primitive slab at Reisk, near Dingle, Co. Kerry, which bears a cross having the head formed of circular arcs and the shaft of spirals.   The stone is inscribed ōne.   The head of this cross may be compared with Nos. 24, 25, Plates XIX. and XX.

In Plate XII. three smaller stones are shown; the first (A) is from Iniskea North, Co. Mayo; it is broken and is now about 4 ft. 6 in. by 3 ft. On it is a crucifixion of primitive type, with sponge and spear bearers.   Its early date is marked by the spirals placed on the legs of the central figure. The crucifixion is the only scene represented on monuments of this kind and that very rarely; sometimes there is an ornamental cross with a figure at either side as shown in Plate X. and in No. 55, Plates XXV. and XXVI.

The second stone, (B) from Caherlehillan, Co. Kerry, is 3 ft. 5 in. in height and 1 ft. 4 in. in breadth.   Like the Reisk slab it bears a cross formed of circular arcs, and has the rare addition of a bird symbol placed above the cross as well as two curved lines below; the latter may represent serpents.   The bird is possibly a dove, but is more probably a phœnix as emblem of the Resurrection.

The third (C) is portion of a broken pillar stone, 2 ft. 11 in. by 10 in., at Cliffony, Co. Sligo.   The design is of interest not only on account of the Swastika, which may be compared with those in Figure 9, but also of the concentric circles and saltires resembling those often seen on Pre-Christian monuments.

Plate XIII. contains a series of the small unshaped stones which are the most numerous class of early sepulchral monuments.   Inscriptions,

---

[9] Dr. J. U. Macnamara, *Journal R.S.A.I.*, vol. xxix. (1899), p. 246.

it will be noticed, hold a more important place on these stones than on the crosses or standing stones. The small slabs (A) and (B) are examples of the Greek crosses in use about the year 800.[10] (A)—Clonmacnois, No. 19, 16 in. by 11½ in.—has a small plain cross with enlarged ends, and is inscribed ᚱⁿeⴅⱁⱒeⴀᵹⱁⱅ.[11] (B)—Inis Cealtra, No. 27, 27 in. × 15 in.—has the cross enclosed in a square panel decorated with frets and knots. Circular panels were also used; they are sufficiently illustrated in Plates XIX. and XX., and in Figure 4. (C)—Inisbofinne, Co. Westmeath—21 in. by 14 in., shows a ringed cross similar in outline to the high crosses, it is inscribed ⱞⴀeⱅⱞⴀⱋⱅⴀⰹⱀ, and probably belongs to the ninth century.

(D)—Clonmacnois, No. 68, 26 in. × 24 in.—bears a ringed cross of four lines in a square panel decorated with a border of Greek fret. The design seems transitional between (B) and (C).

(E)—Clonfert, 33 in. × 24 in.—has on it a three line cross with expanded centre and extremities. Two patterns contained in them are shown at C and H, Figure 8. Crosses of this type belong to the tenth century.[12] The Inscription consists only of the name ⰱeⲥᵹⴀⱀ.

(F)—Clonmacnois, No. 168, 3 ft. 4 in. × 21 in.[13]—is a variety of the last type. The cross is formed of one band which at the centre interlaces with a circle, and at the ends forms triquetra-like knots. The inscription reads o̅ⱃ ⴅⱁ ⴅⴀⰹⱀeⰹⱅ, the letters being exceptionally well shaped. A handsome device of this type from Lemanaghan, King's County, is shown in Dr. Petrie's *Christian Inscriptions*,[14] and a more elaborate example from Inismurray in Wakeman's *Survey*.[15]

(G)—Clonmacnois, No. 192, 22 in. × 14 in.—is a roughly rectangular slab on which is incised a cross like that shown at E, but having the addition of loops at the angles. These loops mark a later period, most likely the beginning of the eleventh century. The inscription is in two lines reading downwards, o̅ⱃ ⴀⱃ ᵹⰹⱅⱅⴀᵹⰹⴀⱋⴀⰹⱀ.

Plate XIV. contains three examples of more highly decorated sepulchral slabs. (A) Tullylease, 38 in. × 24 in.—shows a cross of the type having expanded centre and extremities, with spirals at the angles of the latter; it is arranged to combine the Greek and Latin forms. The decoration is good and consists of an all-over diagonal fret with an interlaced knot in the centre. In the quarters are circles containing frets united with spirals. These designs are greatly injured, as pilgrims visiting the stone rub them with a pebble while offering prayers. See I., Figure 3, and E, Figure 6.

The inscription is Latin in Irish characters: qui cum quᴀe ⱒunc ⱅⰹⱅuⱡú ⱡeᵹeⱃⰹⱅ oⱃⴀⱅ ⱒⱃo ⰱeⱃeⱒⱅuⰹⱃe.[16]

<hr>

[10] Dr. R. A. S. Macalister, *Proceedings, Royal Irish Academy*, vol. xxxiii., Sect. C., p. 150.

[11] According to the *Annals* an Abbot of Clonmacnois, thus named, died in 781.

[12] Dr. R. A. S. Macalister, as last referred to.

[13] The blank portion of the stone is omitted to save space; the cross is 11½ inches in length.

[14] Vol. i., Plate lii.

[15] Page 98, Fig. 46.

[16] St. Beretchert died in the year 839.

In the upper angle are the Greek characters $\overline{\chi\rho\varsigma}$ which probably corresponded to $\overline{\iota\eta\varsigma}$ at the other angle, now broken away. A cross of exactly the same shape occupies an ornamental page at the beginning of St. Matthew's Gospel in the *Book of Lindisfarne*.[17]

(B)—Durrow Abbey, 43 in. × 16 in.—is a handsome tenth century slab transitional between the types shown at C and E, Plate XIII. It has the ring as well as the enlarged centre and ends: the ring is decorated with spirals and the ends, except the top, with knots. The extremities are in this case rectangular, with the exception of the top which is semicircular. The inscription is óṗ ꝺo ᚐiꝿroiu.

(C)—Clonmacnois, No. 81, 45 in. × 43 in.—is the best design of the Clonmacnois series; as a photograph was not available it has been drawn from a rubbing.   The design consists of a circular panel, edged with key-pattern and containing a very original cruciform device formed of knot-work. The centrepiece is worn away, and is shown restored after Dr. Macalister;[18] no other pattern fits the existing traces. The inscription is well cut and reads:—Óṗ ᚐṗ ꝼiᚐchṗᚐich. There was a Fiachra connected with Clonmacnois in the beginning of the tenth century and this is probably his monument.

CAREFUL comparison of the designs carved on such monuments as the foregoing indicates that their most striking characteristics are, in the first place, the closeness with which, in spite of endless variety, they adhere to certain types; and in the second their limitations, that is, the number of possible forms which were not used.

The artists who worked at the decoration of monuments and other objects evidently preferred, or were expected, to confine themselves to certain well-established motives or conventions; but were free, so long as these were clearly rendered, to modify the arrangement and proportions as they chose. These pecularities cause the designs to fall naturally into distinct classes, which are in most cases kept separate, though sometimes combined in one pattern. When the latter happens, the portions which belong to each motive can at once be recognised. The tailpiece to the first chapter is an instance.

The primary division is, according to form, into *Abstract or Geometrical Designs and Biomorphic or Living Forms*. According to the meaning the divisions are, *Decorative*, *Symbolic*, and *Pictorial Designs*.

This latter principle introduces the difficulty that, in many cases it is uncertain whether there is a specific meaning or merely an effort to please the eye in general; and that many of the pictorial designs have a secondary

---

[17] Illustrated by the Rev. Stanford F. H. Robinson in *Celtic Illuminative Art;* also in the British Museum, *Book of Lindisfarne.*
[18] *Memorial Slabs of Clonmacnois*, pp. 16 and 108.

symbolic meaning. For the practical purpose of illustrating the different classes of design, it has been found most convenient to deal first with the various types of abstract ornament—*Spiral, Star, Interlaced, and Fret Patterns*, adding a notice of the few geometric forms which are generally thought to have had symbolic meanings: then passing on to *Zoömorphic Ornament* and *Symbols*, and concluding with a number of examples of *Pictorial design.*

DESIGNS ON A BROKEN CROSS AT KILLEANY, ARAN ISLANDS.
(Drawn by the late T. J. Westropp.)

CHAPTER III.

SPIRAL PATTERNS

HEN the ornament formed of spiral curves is examined it proves to be one of the most striking and graceful varieties of geometrical design. It is probably derived from classical scrollwork through the bolder and more flowing spirals of the late Celtic period. The elementary form from which the designs are built up is a curved line with both ends spirally coiled, either in the same or in opposite directions. These variations may be called respectively C and S-curves, and each may have the extremities equal or unequal in size.

The connecting line or band widens out more or less between the coils as a triangle with curved sides; and sometimes has in the centre an oval figure from which comes the name *Trumpet pattern.* The resemblance is, however, more marked in manuscript designs than in carving. The treatment of these expansions is one of the points in which spiral designs differ from each other, and inspection of the illustrations will show that those attached to the S-curves vary more than the others.

Another detail which changes is the shape of the ends; most often they are pear-shaped bulbs, but occasionally several curved bands run in to the centre of the coil and join without thickening. When the number of bands entering a coil is even they are sometimes joined in pairs and form loops near the centre. In some cases the triangular expansion serves as a base from which three spirals start. See A, Figure 11. Spirals can be interlocked in many ways to form effective designs; this will be understood from the illustrations. No. 8, Plates XV. and XVI. may be referred to as one of the most remarkable for simple elegance.

According to Mr. Romilly Allen[1] these patterns are set out by covering the space to be decorated with circles at convenient and fairly equal distances to form a net, connecting them by tangents direct or transverse, and continuing these tangents as spirals inside the circles. As the circles need not be of equal size an irregular space can be covered as easily as one of regular form.

A favourite method of enriching spiral ornament is to raise the centres of some or all of the coils in the shape of rounded bosses. This is clearly seen in the photographs, but the outline drawings do not show it, and the descriptions must be referred to. In rare cases centres are sunk in the form of cups. This happens in two of those shown at A, Figure 11.

---

[1] *Celtic Art*, p. 285.

C and S-curves are used both separately and in combination, thus producing a great range of intricate patterns. Some of the spiral designs are practically identical with corresponding fret patterns, curved lines being used in the one case and straight in the other.

PLATES XV. AND XVI.

No. 1. From the South Cross, Castledermot (15½ in. × 10½ in.).

A simple design of C-shaped curves, formed of two spiral borders placed side by side. The thickening of the central portions of the curves, characteristic of the trumpet pattern, is in this example hardly noticeable.

No. 2. From Boho Cross (18½ in × 9 in.).

Another design of C-shaped curves, in this instance arranged in pairs vertically and horizontally. The small spaces left at the sides are filled by pellets. The design is repeated three times in line on the stone thus showing that, like many other patterns to be illustrated, it is equally suited for use as a border. Two of the repetitions are shown.

No. 3. From Kinnitty Cross (13 in. × 11 in.)

A design similar to the last but duplicated sideways to fill a square, and having the centres of the coils in slight extra relief. The triangular openings left at the sides are filled by small pear-shaped curves instead of the more usual pellets. It will be noticed that the central coil is formed of four spirals, those at the angles of two, and the others of three. By compressing the corners this design is sometimes adapted to a circle, as may be seen on the cross at Old Eglish, near Benburb, Co. Armagh.

No. 4. From the North Cross, Duleek (10½ in. × 4¾ in.).

This pattern resembles No. 2, but the ends are treated differently, and the centres of the spirals form raised bosses. As three spirals cross the ends together there is no room for an expanded portion to the middle one.

No. 5. From Tihilly Cross (10½ in. × 4 in.).

A more elaborate example of spiral design which combines together C and S-shaped curves. In it most of the expansions are pierced, thus showing an approximation towards the oval figures of the manuscripts. As in No. 3, the side spaces are filled by small curves branching off the main spirals.

No. 6. From Tihilly Cross (10¾ in. × 4 in.).

Another design from the same monument as the last, and looking as if it might have been produced by modifying one quarter of No. 5. The central spirals are C-curves having each a large and a small end; and the marginal ones S-curves with both ends small. The ends of the design are differently arranged so as to suit the length of the panel, and any spaces left over are occupied by pellets.

No. 7. From Drumcliff Cross (11 in. × 4 in.).

This panel occupies one segment of the ring, and is a specimen of the rather unusual combination of spiral and interlaced work. The interlacing is more or less in triquetra form and takes the place generally filled by the smaller ends of curves like those in No. 6. Another interesting panel at Drumcliff combines in one design frets, spirals, and knots. A reproduction of it forms the tailpiece to Chapter I.

No. 8.   From Drumcliff Cross (22 in. × 5½ in.).

A very effective design which resembles No. 6, but consists almost entirely of C-curves. There is a curious irregularity where an extra and apparently unnecessary curve is introduced into one of the lower coils. The method of finishing off the ends is also worth noting. This panel is placed upright on the stone, though shown horizontally in the plate; it is suitable for either position.

No. 9.   From the North Cross, Ahenny (16 in. × 5 in.).

A pattern made up of S-curves only, the expanded portions of which are connected round the edge. One would have expected further detail to have been cut on these portions, but the design is perhaps more effective without it.

No. 10.   From Durrow Abbey Cross (2 in. in width).

A border formed of C-curves placed alternately in opposite positions and interlocked. D, Figure 2, shows a similar design from Ahenny; it is, however, of larger size and has the expansions pierced.

No. 11.   From Durrow Abbey Cross (1¾ in. in width).

A spiral border of S-curves with two triangular expansions to each. B, Figure 2, is a similar border of larger size from Kinnitty Cross; it is more elaborate and has small spirals substituted for the triangular parts of the present design.

PLATES XVII. AND XVIII.

No. 12.   From the South Cross, Castledermot (15½ in. × 10 in.)

A plain design of S-curves only, corresponding in part to No. 11, but having the rows of vertical spirals connected above and below by horizontal curves of the same form. The spirals on this cross have hardly a trace of the usual expansions.

No. 13.   From Graiguenamanagh Cross (about 9 in. wide).

A pattern similar to the last, but having vertical and horizontal spirals interlocked with each other all through. There are several panels containing this pattern on the Castledermot crosses, and it appears on the ancient chancel arch of Tuam Cathedral. Designs of the same kind have been found on stone and metal objects of Mycenaean age.

No. 14.   From the North Cross, Ahenny (14 in. × 5 in.).

One half of a long panel of typical trumpet-pattern formed of S-curves. The arrangement is that not uncommon one in which two spirals lie side by side from end to end, and have their expanded parts on opposite sides, the latter thus filling the intervals between the coils. The way in which the lines of the expansions are managed is very good; also the modification by which three and not four curves enter the coils other than those at the ends.

No. 15. From the North Cross, Ahenny (10¾ in. × 6 in.).

This example belongs to the class of unsymmetrical designs in which the elements of the pattern follow each other in the same direction. The expanded portions of the curves are triangular or harp-shaped, and are connected round the margin. In the centre four spirals meet and unite in pairs. The border round this panel is a good example of the cable or rope moulding often used.

No. 16. From Bealin Cross (11¼ in. × 8¾ in.).

. A design of mixed C and S-curves which resembles one element of No. 5, but consists of two C and four S-curves only. It is a symmetrical pattern and illustrates further modifications of the expanded portions of spirals; those of the C-curves having projections shaped like spear-heads, which assist in filling the spaces between the coils. The design is repeated on a cross-shaft at Clonmacnois.

No. 17. From Muiredach's Cross, Monasterboice (9¾ in. × 8 in).

A fine example of mixed curves terminating on hemispherical bosses. The lines appear to have been cut to a less depth as they approach the centres; and as these parts, being raised, are very exposed, the spiral ends have been worn away. They are restored from analogy with many others.

No. 18. From Muiredach's Cross, Monasterboice (21 in. × 11 in.).

A more complex and better preserved pattern of the same class as No. 17, in which many of the spirals can be traced to their centres. The expansions are pierced with plain parallel openings. The manner in which the spirals connect the bosses and fill the spaces between is remarkable for its freedom and variety. This, as well as No. 17, illustrates the treatment of the marginal spirals in designs containing bosses; some being left flat and reduced in size through lack of space. The corner pieces of the panel cannot be made out with certainty; they differ in shape from the other coils, and may possibly be animal heads introduced in the manner seen in No. 76.

No. 19. From the West Cross, Kells (18½ in. × 10 in.).

An effective design, arranged to have the space between the central curves cruciform. This is an idea often worked out in interlacing and sometimes in fret patterns, but rarely in spirals. The expansions are again treated differently, and the coils are connected in an unusual manner.

No. 20. From the South Cross, Clonmacnois (21¾ in. × 13½ in.).

This is a design which in its worn state looks similar to Nos. 17 and 18, but on close examination proves to have bosses covered with interlacing— a doubtful improvement. It is uncertain whether all the bosses were decorated with the same pattern, but it is probable that they were, and they are so restored. The bosses nearest to the top of the panel retain sufficient traces of the design to show that it consisted of three separate rings interlaced together; two being ovals crossed diagonally, and the third having four closed loops disposed as a quatrefoil. One of the bosses is shown on a larger scale in No. 20A, Plates XXV. and XXVI.

FIGURE 2.—SPIRAL BORDERS.

A. From Durrow Abbey Cross (12 in. × 2½ in.).

This is on one of the segments of the ring; it is much broken and worn, and only the first half can be made out; this is, however, sufficient to allow of restoration. Like J, Figure 7, the design is a combination of frets and spirals, but here the latter take up a greater proportion of the space. The central part of the border is filled by stepped lines placed in squares, and the edges by the spirals. There is also something of the key pattern in the arrangement of the bands which connect the steps and spirals.

B. From Kinnitty Cross (13½ in. × 3 in.).

A closely coiled spiral border made up of unequal-ended C-curves in pairs; each joined to the next by a small S-curve placed crosswise. In No. 11 a small border of the same kind is shown; it is simplified by the omission of the S-curves.

C. From Killameary Cross (15½ in. × 3½ in.).

A spiral border in which the S-curves are sunk, leaving continuous triangular figures in relief. No. 9 is a variation of the same idea.

D. From the South Cross, Ahenny (19 in. × 3 in.).

An effective design of C-curves with plain voided expansions interlocked together in a single row. The pattern is an open one and larger spaces than usual are left unfilled. One would have expected them to have been occupied by pellets, or by lozenges connected with the points of the expansions after the manner seen in B, Figure 11.

E. From the North Cross, Ahenny (17¼ in. × 3¼ in.).

A border consisting of closely coiled S-curves interlocked in pairs, and arranged to have a curve start from each of the three angles of the triangular expansions instead of from two only as usual. The design is a more highly developed variety of that shown at C.

F. From Muiredach's Cross, Monasterboice (20 in. × 4 in.).

A more complex border than the preceding, it consists of large three-fold spiral coils placed centrally and alternating with sets of four smaller coils arranged in squares. The spirals, chiefly C-curves, are placed in such a way that three converge to every centre except to those at the ends. This design is carved on alternate segments of the ring, the intervening segments having a similar pattern in which the large coils are separated by two instead of four smaller ones.

FIGURE 3.—CIRCULAR AND SEMICIRCULAR
SPIRAL PATTERNS.

A. From the South Cross, Ahenny (5 in. diameter).

A small pattern of three centres connected by S-curves. It is carved on one of the bosses, and surrounded by two concentric rings.

B. From Slab No. 189 at Clonmacnois (5 in. diameter).

A design of four centres joined by C-curves arranged in an unusual way. Two of the curves are above and two below the centres which they

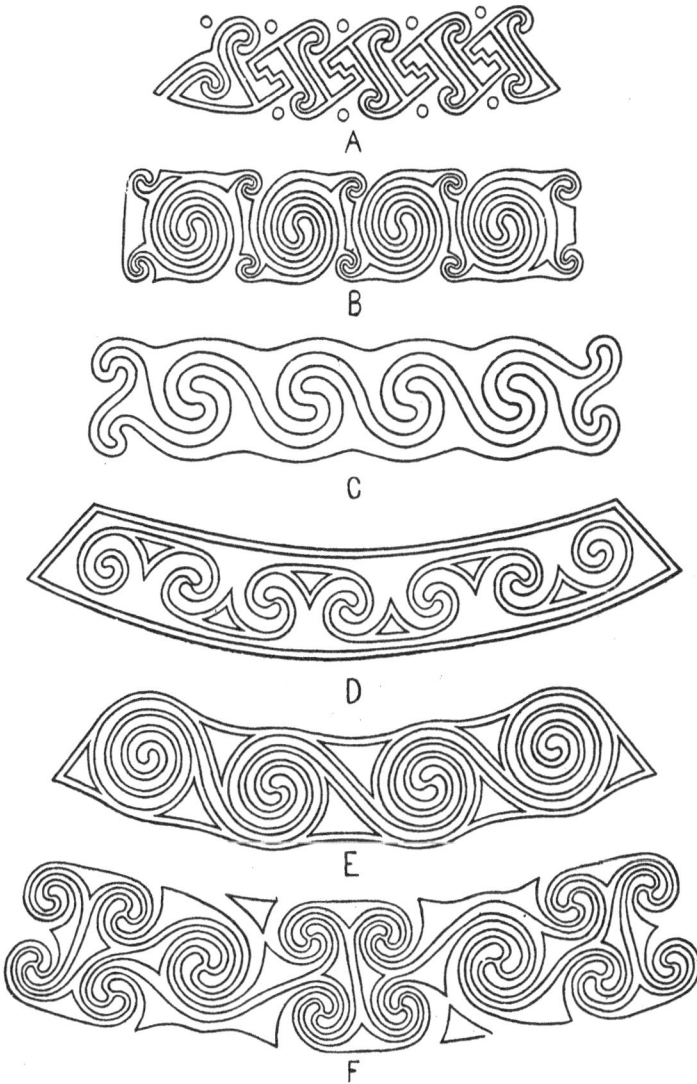

FIG. 2.—SPIRAL BORDERS.

connect. The outer curves touch along the horizontal diameter, and are joined together to form a complete circle.

C. From a slab at Clonfert (7¼ in. × 4¼ in.).

A design of the same kind as B, but shaped to fill a semicircle. The vacant spaces are filled by pellets.

D. From a cross at Tynan Abbey (10¼ in. diameter).

A cruciform design in which eight coils are placed round the circle and connected by C-curves alternately inside and out. The latter curves are joined to the uncarved space in the centre so as to form a cross.

FIG. 3.—CIRCULAR AND SEMICIRCULAR SPIRAL PATTERNS.

E. From Slab No. 157 at Clonmacnois (8 in. diameter).

A central coil surrounded by six others in pairs, all of the latter are joined by C-curves and three of them are connected with the centre. The design is found on five or six slabs at Clonmacnois and on one at Inis Cealtra; modifications of it are carved on several High Crosses. Compare G, given below.

F. From a slab at Durrow Abbey (5½ in. × 3½ in.).

A pattern of the same kind as E but shaped to fit a semicircle. Spirals are not often placed in semicircles, and this instance is not very successful. The complete slab is shown in Plate XIV.

G. From Kinnitty Cross (10 in. diameter).

This is a variety of E which has the central coil larger than the others, and all the coils raised as bosses. The outer coils are equally spaced and connected by S-curves. The stone is in bad condition and the cutting on the expanded portions of the spirals is uncertain; it is given as nearly as it can be ascertained.

H. From the North Cross, Monasterboice (10 in. diameter).

This design has in all sixteen coils, twelve of which are placed round the circumference and four round the centre. It is really an adaptation to a circle of the standard repetition pattern of C-curves. If all the curves were present four elements would enter each of the central coils; as there is hardly room for this, one curve is omitted at each side.

I. From a slab at Tullylease (5¼ in. diameter).

This is an interesting design in which frets and spirals are united. It belongs to the class which has a central coil and eight others ranged equally round it. In this example four of the outer coils are changed to fret or key pattern. In other cases, for instance on the cross at Eglish in Armagh, all the spirals are present. A similar design in a square panel is given in No. 3, Plates XV. and XVI.

DESIGN RESTORED FROM A BROKEN CROSS-SLAB AT CLONMACNOIS. (1/8.)

CHAPTER IV.

STAR PATTERNS

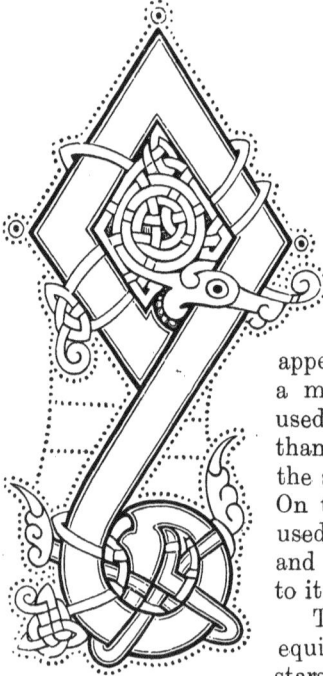

UITE a different effect is produced when the circles forming the net on which spiral patterns are constructed are allowed to intersect; the designs then take a star-like appearance. These star or radial patterns form a minor division of Celtic ornament; they are used less frequently and admit of fewer variations than the other types. In these notes they follow the spirals, as both are formed on nets of circles. On the monuments the simplest forms only are used—those on which the circles are of one radius and have their centres spaced at distances equal to it.

The centres may be placed at the angles of equilateral triangles or of squares. Six-rayed stars are produced by the former arrangement, and four-rayed by the latter. In the six-ray pattern the rays are independent, but in the four-ray they intersect and are generally interlaced as shown in No. 28. Several modifications and ornamental forms are shown in Figure 4. The six-ray pattern does not lend itself to modification, and there are apparently no decorated examples in Ireland; unless that shown in No. 23 can be excepted. Mr. Romilly Allen has illustrated a Scottish example from Argyle[1] which is enriched with spirals in a manner analogous to D, Figure 4.

Star patterns do not seem to have been used as borders, though it is evident that they might readily be adapted to that purpose. Nos. 27 and 28 for instance only require repetition to form effective borders, and the same applies to No. 29, which is actually made up of two borders combining radial and interlaced designs.

Several of the most characteristic types of cross are formed of circular arcs, and being thus closely connected with radial patterns are illustrated with them. Designs like Nos. 21, 22, 24, have all been worn as ornaments on St. Patrick's Day.[2]

---

[1] In *Early Christian Monuments of Scotland*, part iii., p. 401.
[2] *Journal, Cork Hist. and Arch. Society*, vol. i., second series (1895), p. 555.

PLATES XIX. AND XX.

No. 21. From Ardane Cross (7½ in. diameter).

A six-rayed star pattern which fills the centre of the larger cross-head at Ardane, near Bansha. In this case the star is single and complete, without the extra rays which in some examples lie round the enclosing circle, and which No. 22 shows clearly to be portions of other overlapping stars.

This is one of the most easily constructed of geometrical patterns, being entirely set out by compass without alteration of radius; on this account possibly it has always remained in use, and may be seen on medieval monuments as well as on those of early date. In modern times it has been worn on St. Patrick's Day. The use of this design may originally have been connected with that form of the Sacred Monogram which is composed of the Greek initials I and X; when these are combined and placed in a circle a wheel with six spokes is produced.[3]

No. 22. From Slab No. 82 at Clonmacnois (14 in. diameter).

This design is similar to the last but continuous, the pattern formed by intersecting arcs of circles being repeated all over a circle of 14 in. diameter. The stars, whose centres lie on or near this circle, would necessarily have two rays outside it; these rays are suppressed and replaced by one of smaller size which lies on the surrounding border. It is difficult to understand why two rays were not carved instead of one, they would have lain obliquely on the border and might, therefore, have more nearly approached the inner rays in size.

No. 23. From an erect slab at Carndonagh (33½ in. × 15½ in.).

A handsome design, having a star of *seven rays* surrounded by a circular band which at the base forms a long stem with a double looped termination. The rays proceeding from the centre and those placed round the circumference are hollowed out or *voided;* outside the circle and in the centre are pellets similarly treated, while smaller pellets occupy the intervals between the rays.

The stem is ornamented by a key-pattern arranged to form a small cross about half-way down; on either side is placed a rude figure (not shown) rather like those in No. 55, Plates XXV. and XXVI. It is impossible to cover a space geometrically with seven-rayed stars or heptagons, and it is probable that this star is a modification of the six-rayed pattern intended to bring in the symbolism of the number seven.

No other design exactly like this is known, and it can only be compared to those on slabs at Iniskea and Reisk. These have four-ray patterns or crosses like No. 24 enclosed in circles and placed on spiral stems. Some of the carvings on pillar-stones at Glencolumbkille have a slight resemblance in general outline to this one, and the same applies to two designs drawn by Mr. Wakeman from Inismurray.[4]

No. 24. From a pillar-stone at Clone (12 in. diameter).

An incised cross formed of circular arcs. This design is frequently

---

[3] F. E. Hulme, *Symbolism in Christian Art,* p. 50.
[4] *Antiquarian Remains on the Island of Inismurray,* pp. 104-6.

used both as a cross and as an ornament; Nos. 27, 28, 29 are examples of the latter use. The figure is formed of arcs struck from four equidistant points on the circumference of a circle of the same radius. When used as a cross the arcs do not project beyond the circle, but as ornament they are often produced to meet in a point outside.

No. 25. From Slab No. 24 at Inis Cealtra (11 in. diameter).

A design similar to the last but ornamented by double-band triquetras in the cross arms; and by having the arcs continued and bent into patterns in the alternate divisions. The curved bands lend themselves well to interlacing, and are often treated in that way both at the centre and at the circumference. This interlacing, however, is not a necessary part of the design, and is sometimes absent as in the last example and in the design from Glendalough given at C, Figure 4. Similar designs are found in the ornamental pages of the *Book of Durrow*, especially that facing the beginning of St. Mark's Gospel.

No. 26. From an erect slab at Carndonagh (23 in. × 16 in.)

An example of a star pattern, the rays of which are interlaced and completed outside the circle. In this instance the circle is divided at the base and the ends worked into a key pattern.

No. 27. From Killamery Cross (25 in. × 12½ in.).

Two of the three repetitions of a four-rayed star pattern carved on the shaft of the cross. (The head of this cross is shown in No. 96.) In this design the circles or rings are omitted and the spaces between the rays filled by triangles and diamonds; the upper one being cut into a triquetra and the central into a swastika of the kind sometimes called *Chinese*. Compare C, Figure 9, which shows a similar swastika from Clonmacnois.

No. 28. From Killeany Cross (11½ in. × 7½ in.).

A panel bearing a continuous pattern of four-rayed stars like that in No. 26. As already mentioned, patterns of this class are usually interlaced, and in this instance it is of interest to note that one of the interlacings is incorrect. The design could, of course, be formed, like other interlaced work, by modifying a plait, but in this case the simpler device of intersecting arcs is available, and the interlacing is probably an ornamental addition. The inaccuracy is further evidence of this; as such irregularities are not found in the ordinary interlaced patterns though they are occasionally in Zoömorphic designs, where, as here, the crossing of the bands is not the only consideration.[5]

The panel from which No. 28 is taken was originally square, but one-third is now broken away. The same pattern is found on the base of Ullard Cross, where it consists of four divisions only. It decorates one side of the leather satchel of the Shrine of St. Moedoc,[6] and appears in metalwork on the Cumdach of Dimma's Gospels.[7]

---

[5] See No. 91, Plates xxxiii. and xxxiv., and B, Figure 10.

[6] Illustrated in the *Guide to the Antiquities of the Christian Period, in the Royal Irish Academy Collection*, p. 52.

[7] Illustrated in the *Transactions of the Royal Irish Academy*, vol. xiii., part iii., p. 175.

No. 29. From the West Cross, Kilkieran (17½ in. × 12 in.).

This panel gives further information as to the combining of interlaced and radiating designs. The upper and lower portions are distinct, each being part of a border or repetition pattern. The upper section is made up of three four-rayed stars like No. 26, the surrounding circles being connected as a twist, and the rays completed outside. The sculptor has introduced a decided irregularity in the central portion. In the lower section there are two six-rayed stars on circular plaques, separated by knotwork which partially surrounds them. Either of these sections, if repeated, would produce an effective border.

No. 30. From the West Cross, Kilkieran (6¾ in. × 4½ in.).

This unusual pattern is carved on the end of one of the arms, and as it is deeply sunk and rather worn, it easily escapes notice. It does not elsewhere occur on stone,[8] but is frequently used in the illuminated pages of the *Gospels of Mac Regol*,[9] and fills two small panels on the *Cathac*,[10] now in the Library of the Royal Irish Academy. It may be described as a net of small squares, the diagonals of which are marked; or it may be regarded as an attempt to construct a continuous pattern of eight-rayed stars, a thing which can only be done by altering the lengths of alternate rays so that each star may fit in a square.

No. 31. From Dysert O'Dea Cross (5¼ in. diameter).

One of the rosettes carved, together with some simple leaf-work on the head of the cross. Such floral designs do not generally appear on Irish monuments till a comparatively late date. It is remarkable that a simple form of trumpet pattern is carved between the rosettes; one would have expected it to have disappeared long before.[11]

The rosette illustrated has a circular centre surrounded by nine small and nine large petals. At Inis Cealtra there is a large Romanesque slab with a rosette in the centre, this also has nine petals. One of the later slabs at Clonmacnois also has a central rosette with eight petals surrounded by sixteen others.

The small rosettes seen in the *Book of Kells* have eight petals; and the large one which fills the centre of a cross-bearing page in the *Book of Lindisfarne* has a like number. One or two instances of the occurrence of twelve petals may also be found in the *Book of Kells*.

FIGURE 4.—STAR PATTERNS AND CROSSES.

A. From the South Cross, Ahenny (5½ in. diameter).

A star of six rays carved on a projecting boss; it is similar to No. 21, with the addition of marginal rays like those seen in Nos. 22 and 23.

---

[8] That is in Ireland; in Scotland it has been found at Oxnam, near Jedburgh:—See *Proceedings, Society of Antiquaries of Scotland*, vol. xxxix. (1904-5), p. 53. In Rome it is carved on the early chancels (screens) in the oratory of Equezio and in the Church of St. Lorenzo :—See Lowrie's *Monuments of the Early Church*, p. 167.

[9] *Proceedings, Royal Irish Academy*, vol. xxix., Sect. C., Plates 1-4.

[10] *Same*, vol. xxxiii., Sect. C., Plate 37.

[11] Illustrated in the *Journal, Royal Society of Antiquaries of Ireland*, vol. xxix. (1899), p. 253.

B. From the West Cross, Kilkieran (6 in. diameter).

This is an enlarged drawing of one of the star patterns shown in No. 29. It resembles A, except that the background is not hollowed out.

C. From a broken slab at St. Kevin's, Glendalough (9½ in. diameter).

A cross formed of circular arcs like No. 24, but ornamented by the re-duplication of lines. At the ends of the arms are oval figures which have no meaning as connected with this class of design, but which may be introduced on the analogy of those seen in the six-ray patterns of which they form an integral part.

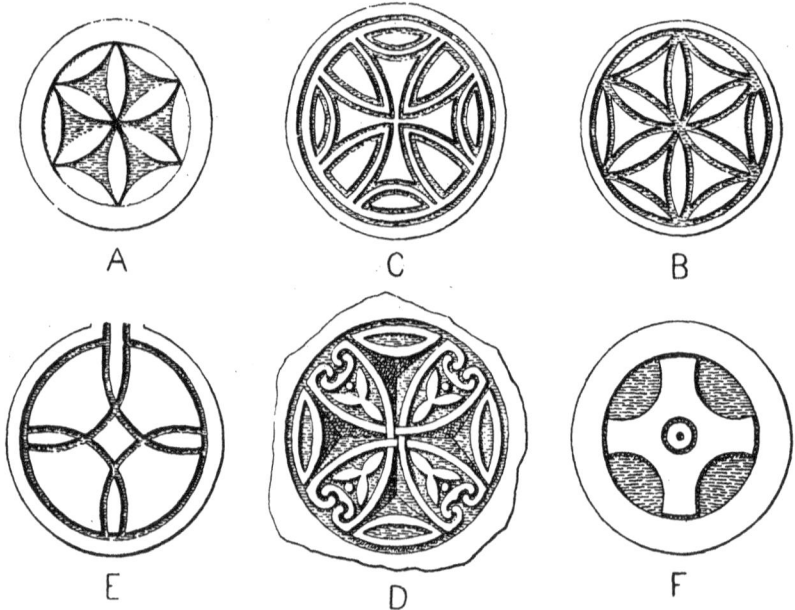

FIG. 4.—STAR PATTERNS AND CROSSES.

D. From Slab No. 22 at Inis Cealtra (15 in. diameter).

A cross of the same kind as the last mentioned, but decorated by spirals, pellets and elongated trefoils.

E. From a slab at Clonburren (6 in. diameter).

The lower extremity of a cross with circularly expanded terminals. The design is formed by shortening the radii of the arcs so that they do not reach the centre of the circle; the figure is also rotated through 45 degrees. A similar design is cut on Slab No. 76 at Clonmacnois.

F. From a Cross at Rhefert Church, Glendalough (12 in. diameter).

In this case the arcs are struck with a radius so short that they do not intersect, and in this way a cross of different type is produced. A further modification of the standard design is occasionally made by enlarging the circle—such as that shown in No. 26—so as to enclose the outer points of the rays.

CHAPTER V.

INTERLACED PATTERNS

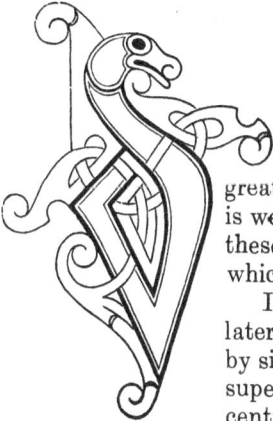

ESIGNS formed of bands interlaced or plaited together are more frequently used and exhibit a greater variety than any others. Ornament of this kind is well known in Italy and the east of Europe, and from these sources the Celts, no doubt, obtained the idea which they developed with so much genius.

Interlaced patterns came into use at a somewhat later date than spirals, and though they were used side by side for a considerable time, the latter were gradually superseded, and are not often found after the tenth century. The patterns consist of bands crossing each other alternately over and under and present two principal classes—plaits and knots. In the plaits each band passes through the pattern from side to side before turning back, but in knotted patterns the bands frequently turn back in the body of the design.

Plaited designs do not present any great variety though they may have different numbers of strands and be shaped to fit irregular panels. From them, nevertheless, are formed the endless kinds of knotwork, by simply dividing some of the bands where they cross, and joining up the ends in different pairs. This process by which—aided by changes in the shape of the loops—the various types of pattern have been evolved, is explained at great length in *The Early Christian Monuments of Scotland*,[1] and more shortly in *Celtic Art*.[2]

When the cuttings or breaks in the bands are far apart the *plaited* effect does not altogether disappear, and the result is known as broken plait. When nearer together the various forms of knot are produced, not only by the relative positions of the breaks, but by alterations in the curves of the bands. Well marked classes are *pointed*, *triangular* and *circular* knotwork, the first and third of which are very characteristic of Irish monuments, but the second is hardly seen except at Kilfenora.

Many interlaced designs are enriched by a line incised along the centre of the band, and there are several in Donegal which have two lines placed near the edges of a broad band. Something of the same kind is seen in metal on the well-known Ballyspellane brooch, but there the bands seem to form part of conventionalised animal patterns. True two-band patterns are also fairly common and easily distinguished from the above, even when the bands are close together, by the fact that the bands separate when they cross a third; one passing over and the other under it.

---

[1] Part ii., pp. 145-201.   [2] Pp. 259-278.

Having got as far as a band provided with borders it is strange that three-band patterns are unknown; for it would only be necessary to equalise the divisions to form a threefold band,[3] and to reverse all the crossings of the central division to obtain three distinct bands.

PLATES XXI. AND XXII.

No. 32. From the West Cross, Kilkieran. (12½ in. × 9 in.)
Half of a panel of plait-work from the base of the Cross. The complete design consists of four separate and similar plaits which leave a narrow cruciform space between them.

No. 33. From Clonca Cross. (21 in. × 13 in.)
Portion of a plaited design in which the band has an incised line along the centre. This double band is frequently seen and should be carefully distinguished from the true two-band pattern shown in No. 40. In this panel the band is not closed but ends at the lower right-hand corner and begins at the upper corner on the same side (not shown). This incompleteness is caused by the uneven number of strands in the plait; if there had been one more or one less in the width, the ends would have joined.

No. 34. From the South Cross, Ahenny. (12½ in. wide.)
This is a good example of plaited ornament of the open variety which allows the background to appear through the pattern. It also illustrates the way in which a plait can be modified to suit a narrowing panel, and how twists are used in places where there is little space. The band in this, as in the last instance, is double and is carried over the entire cross-head without a break.

No. 35. From the West Cross, Kilkieran. (17½ in. × 12 in.)
A curiously irregular design the peculiarity of which is that while three-quarters are quite similar and plain, the fourth is so different as to produce a strong contrast and want of balance. The sculptor has not, however, interfered with the central opening which remains complete in the form of a Latin cross with expanded ends. In the plate the design is placed upright for convenience, but on the stone it is horizontal, the irregular part being at the lower right-hand corner.

No. 36. From the North Cross, Ahenny. (11 in. wide.)
Portion of an excellent pattern of broken plait which covers the whole head of the cross. Here and there in it may be observed places where the strands instead of crossing are broken and joined up so as to turn back. In the centre of the upper part are seen horizontal and vertical *breaks* of this kind. This illustration shows also how such a pattern can be gracefully carried round a boss or other impediment. This pattern is more fully shown in Plate LI.

---

[3] A well-cut pattern of *late date* with a three-fold band, may be noticed on an armorial stone built into the face of the old church tower at Kells, Co. Meath.

No. 37. From Emlagh Cross. (12 in. wide.)

This is one of the simplest forms of knotted pattern, and is made from a six cord plait by cutting and bending the strands alternately at the centre and edges. A good example of this pattern may be seen on the High Cross of Kilfenora. For a full discussion of the evolution of knotwork, Mr. Romilly Allen's works must be consulted.

No. 38. From Bealin Cross. (12 in. × 8 in.)

A further example of broken plait. Four breaks only are made and the bands slightly curved, yet the result gives the impression of knots linked together at the top, centre, and base. It is this process of cutting bands, joining them up differently, and altering their shapes which gives rise to all the varieties of knotted patterns.

No. 39. From Bealin Cross. (12½ in. × 8 in.)

A common variety of knotwork which may perhaps be distinguished as *pointed*, since one extremity of each knot or hitch runs to a sharp angle. The pattern is formed of two distinct bands, each of which makes alternate knots and passes straight through the others.

No. 40. From Kinnitty Cross. (12½ in. × 12½ in.)

The same kind of knotwork as the last, but formed of two bands placed side by side. These bands pass one over and one under each strand which they meet; in contrast to those like Nos. 33 and 34, which may be considered to have one band with a mark along the centre.

PLATES XXIII. and XXIV.

No. 41. From a Slab at Gallen Priory. (4½ in. × 1½ in.)

A complete twist used by itself to fill a small panel.

No. 42. From a Slab at Ardane. (2¼ in. wide.)

Portion of a twist having a double band.

No. 43. From the North Cross, Duleek. (6¾ in. × 6¾ in.)

A plaited design of almost unique form, there seems to be no other instance in which straight bands lie in three directions at approximately equal angles, and thus produce what may be called *triangular* interlacing.

Mr. Romilly Allen points out that interlacing, and ornament in general, can be set out on the *square* or on the *triangular* system; and states that the former only is used in Celtic decoration.[4] To the last statement this panel might seem an exception, but it appears preferable to bring it under the square system by adding to the two sets of diagonal guide lines of the ordinary plait a third, making angles of 45° with them. The actual angles in the design lie between the two systems.

No. 44. From the North Cross, Duleek. (7 in. × 6¼ in.)

This panel is from the same monument as No. 43 and occupies the position corresponding to it on the other arm. The design is a variety

---

[4] *Early Christian Monuments of Scotland*, part ii., p. 132.

of pointed knotwork in which the knots are in pairs and have two angular extremities; thus closely approaching the triangular knotwork in Nos. 47 and 48. A similar design with four double knots in a rectangular panel is carved on the end of one arm of the Durrow Cross, and a circular variety of the same from Clonmacnois is given at D, Figure 6.

No. 45.   From Termonfechin Cross.   (15½ in. × 5¼ in.)

An example of pointed knotwork in which the knots are arranged in pairs surrounded by an outer band; the points of each pair being at opposite sides.   The lower end is modified as the panel is too short to admit of a complete repetition.   This pattern approaches in effect the circular knotwork shown below.

No. 46.   From Tihilly Cross.   (10½ in. × 4 in.)

A variety of knotted pattern which shows a double band and has the loops bent in the form of the letter S instead of being pointed at one end and crossed at the other as in the last example.   In addition two of these S-shaped curves are interlaced with each other instead of having one strand looped and the other passing straight through.   The lower part is modified as in No. 45.

No. 47.   From the High Cross, Kilfenora.   (11½ in. × 11½ in.)

A characteristic specimen of *triangular* knotwork, rare in Ireland, but well known in Scotland.   In this striking type of design the bands forming the knots are largely straight and meet in sharp points, thus dividing the field covered by the pattern into triangles.

In this illustration the panel is square and divided cross and saltire-wise; the eight triangles being each filled by a knot.   The design shown is one of two which are connected.

No. 48.   From the High Cross, Kilfenora.   (12½ in. × 11½ in.)

This is a more intricate piece of triangular interlacing from the same monument.   The main division is into four parts, but the whole surface is also divided into sixteen small triangles each containing a knot.   The knots at each corner are connected by circular loops which pass twice round.

No. 49.   From Drumcliff Cross.   (17 in. × 10 in.)

One of the simplest forms of *circular knotwork*, so called because the principal lines are curved in circular or spiral shape.   It has a great resemblance to the pointed knotwork in No. 39, but there is an additional circular turn round each knot, and the pointed parts are rounded off.   The band is not complete, it should have another strand across the lower edge to connect the loose ends.

No. 50.   From Boho Cross.   (20 in. × 9½ in.)

This is a more complex instance of circular knotwork, in which pointed loops are grouped in sets of four, surrounded by two concentric rings. The ends of the panel are filled by twists.   Complete circular rings are unusual, generally they are cut, and the ends joined to the other interlacing.   Continued repetition of this design would produce a satisfactory border.

No. 51.   From an erect Slab at Carndonagh.   (26 in. × 16½ in.)

A cross decorated with interlacing; the stem and arms are covered with twists which end in triquetras above and below.   The cross stands on a base of key-pattern, and thus unites in one design interlacing and fretwork.

PLATES XXV. AND XXVI.

No. 52.   From Muiredach's Cross, Monasterboice.   (21 in. × 11½ in.)

This design and the following are specimens of the most elaborate kinds of circular knotwork.   Each contains six complete knots and two half knots so as to suit the available space.   In this panel each knot has two strands passing through diagonally, and two concentric circles; the outer of which makes two large loops at the top, and the inner two small ones at the base.   The moulding round the panel is interesting as it imitates a strap coiled round a rod.

No. 53.   From Muiredach's Cross, Monasterboice.   (21 in. × 11½ in.)

Similar to the last design, but more elaborate; it is perhaps the finest example of its kind.   In it the knots are arranged to have the four loops of the same size, and the enclosing circle in two equal and symmetrical parts.

The spaces between the main knots are filled with small lozenge-shaped figures instead of the usual crossing of strands, and the side spaces with triangles.   In this, as well as in the last design, the band is improved by having a line incised along the centre.

No. 54.   Carndonagh Cross.   (84 in. × 43 in.)

This is a good example of an interlaced cross; it is formed of two bands plaited in the centre and interlaced as triquetras at the extremities. The lower limb is slightly lengthened by an extra twist of the inner band. The upper quarters contain separate triquetras, and the lower birds arranged round centres as triskelia.   On the lower part of the shaft is a device of the kind so often seen in which a human figure is placed between animals or animal-headed figures which are shown as biting the head. Further examples are given in Nos. 99, 100, 101.   On this monument two small figures are added below the animal-headed ones; their feet and those of the central figure are below the present ground level and are not seen in the photograph, but are added in Plate XXVI.

No. 55.   Fahan Cross.   (80 in. × 30 in.)

This monument, which appears to hold an intermediate position between slabs and sculptured crosses, has a splendid cross of interlaced work carved on each face; that shown is the more complex and is hardly equalled by any other.   The form of the design is peculiar; the head is shaped as a Greek cross'with expanding ends, and to this is added a long shaft and base which complete the Latin type of cross.   At either side of the shaft is a rude figure, apparently that of a woman with long hair, and on each figure is an inscription which has not hitherto been deciphered.   The base is hidden by the ground, but is indicated in Plate XXVI.

One of the two bands which make up the head—that which passes nearest to the central boss—forms three triquetras and passes down into the shaft as a twist. The second passes through these triquetras and through the lower part of the Greek cross; while a third is added to complete the shaft and base. Two lines are incised on the bands, the appearance given being that of a central strip with narrow borders. The cross on the other side of this stone has the bands similarly treated; it is illustrated in Plate IX.

No. 20a. From the South Cross, Clonmacnois. (3½ in. diameter.)

This is an enlarged view of the pattern on one of the bosses in the panel shown in No. 20, Plates XVII. and XVIII.; it is given in this Plate for convenience of space. It consists of three separate endless bands interlaced symmetrically.

FIGURE 5.—INTERLACED BORDERS.

A. From the North Cross, Ahenny. (10 in. × 2 in.)

The "Figure of Eight" border, a design frequently used. It is a four-strand plait, every third crossing of which, in the middle line, is cut and the ends joined so as to leave a gap at right angles to the length of the border. If every second crossing were cut another well-known pattern would result, that is, a twist with each crossing surrounded by a ring. Other variations are produced by cutting marginal crossings; some of these are shown in F, which is a pattern of eight strands.

B. From the West Cross, Kilkieran. (10 in. × 2 in.)

A simple twist which fills the segments of the ring. It is on the rings of crosses that ornamental borders are most often carved; on that of the North Cross at Duleek there are eight interlaced patterns, all different.

C. From Muiredach's Cross, Monasterboice. (22 in. × 4 in.)

A six-band plait with cruciform breaks. This is a typical instance of the use of such openings, but being almost out of sight on the upper side of the ring it is seldom noticed by visitors to Monasterboice.

The cruciform openings are formed by cutting the bands at the angles of every fourth central square and joining together diagonal pairs of ends. Saltires could as easily be produced by connecting vertical and horizontal pairs.

D. From Muiredach's Cross, Monasterboice. (20½ in. × 4 in.)

An example of that form of interlacing in which one band is bent twice into a zigzag or S-shape, while the other passes straight through it. In this instance additional richness is obtained by the use of two parallel bands.

E. From the Market Cross, Kells. (16 in. × 3¾ in.)

A handsome pattern of pointed knotwork arranged on the principle mentioned above, that is; one strand is looped and the other passes through to form its loop further on.

F. From the West Cross, Monasterboice. (22½ in. × 3¾ in.)

In this border the design shown at D is further elaborated by making *both* strands form S-curves at the same place, and adding two extra

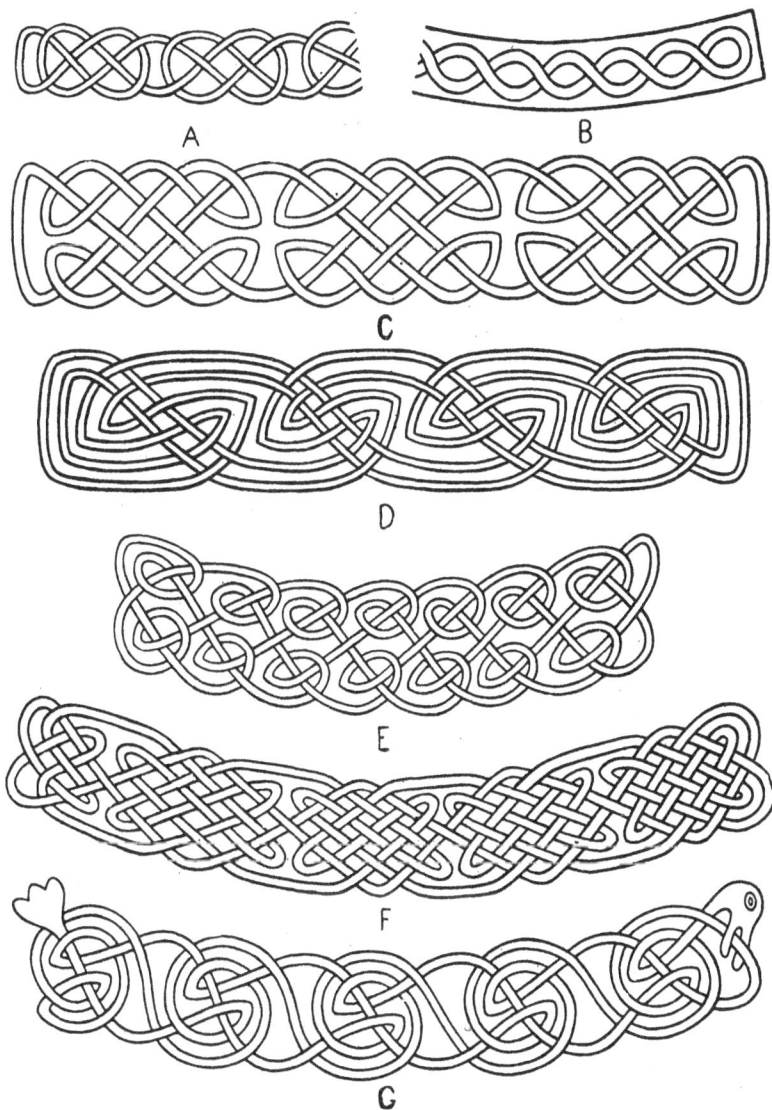

FIG. 5.—INTERLACED BORDERS.

strands which pass through as a twist from end to end. As the space is not completely filled by four knots, a half knot has been introduced at one end. The whole is developed from an eight-strand plait.

G. From the West Cross, Monasterboice. (22 in. × 3½ in.)

This is an example of the use of circular knotwork in a border; it is more often placed in broad panels. As three strands pass from each knot to the next there is necessarily one left over at each end. In a rectangular panel these would probably be joined across the top or base, but in a long narrow design this would be unsatisfactory, and the artist has solved the difficulty by making the loose strands end in a head and tail. The result is thus a connecting link between plain interlaced work and the completely Zoömorphic designs illustrated later on.[5]

FIGURE 6.—CIRCULAR AND OTHER INTERLACED PATTERNS.

A. From Slab No. 163 at Clonmacnois. (5¾ in. × 5¾ in.)

A pattern derived from a square of plait by making four breaks in the centre, and two others unsymmetrically at the sides.

B. From a Slab at Mona Incha. (5½ in. diameter.)

A pattern formed of one circular band with four pointed loops directed towards the centre. The space thus left forms a cross with curved expanding arms; the design is therefore connected with the star or radiating patterns already described.

C. From Bealin Cross. (6 in. diameter.)

This may be looked on as an improvement on the last; the loops are the same, but the connecting portion is split into two bands, each of which passes through the loops formed by the other. In the *Book of Kells* this design is repeated many times, especially on some of the pages of Eusebian Canons. On stone it is seen on the North Cross at Clonmacnois, on Termonfechin Cross and elsewhere.

D. From the South Cross, Clonmacnois. (7½ in. diameter.)

This effective design may be regarded as a development of C; each of the loops there seen being in this case divided.

E. From the Slab of Beretchert at Tullylease. (5½ in. diameter.)

Another development of C, in which the number of the loops is doubled. For the complete slab, see A, Plate XIV.

F. From Termonfechin Cross. (6 in. diameter.)

A design of one band divided into four quadrant-shaped knots; it is often used on sepulchral slabs and other monuments; in many cases the knots have one turn less. See the centre of D, Figure 10.

G. From the South Cross, Duleek. (5½ in. diameter.)

Four triquetras united to produce a cross. Here the cross is small and placed diagonally, but on many slabs it is upright and lengthened out

---

[5] Borders of triangular knotwork have not been found in Ireland, but a typical design of this kind from Bradford-on-Avon Church, Wilts., has been illustrated in the *Journal of the British Archaeological Association*, vol. xxii. (1866), p. 164 and Plate 9.

as a large cross with interlaced ends; there are several examples at Glendalough.[6] Patterns having six triquetras joined are found in the *Book of Kells* but are unknown on stone.

H. From a Cross at Tynan Abbey. ($6\frac{1}{4}$ in. diameter.)

A knot formed of four oval bands interlaced with each other and with

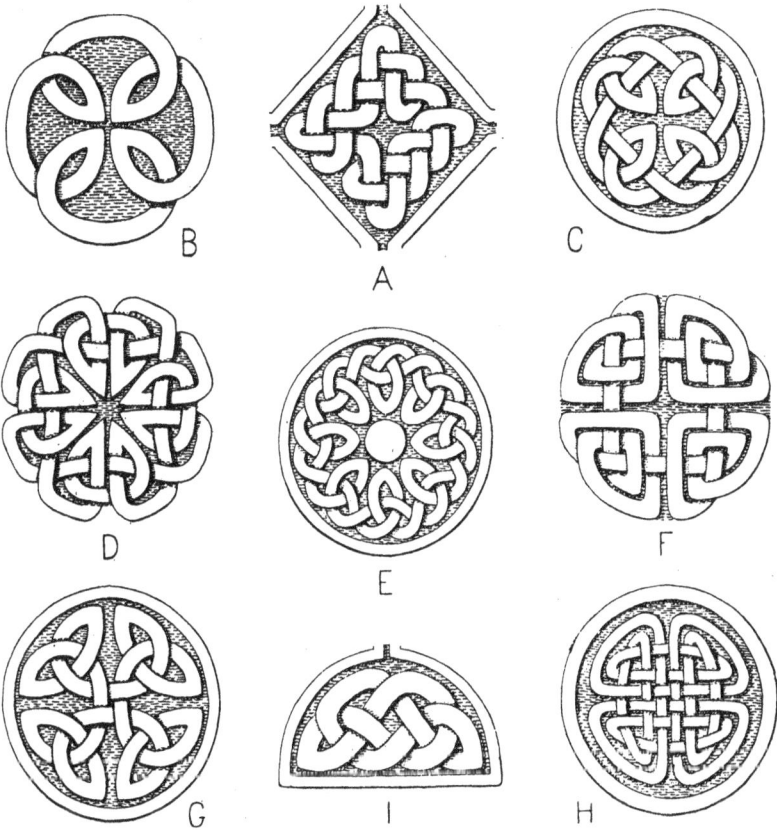

FIG. 6.—CIRCULAR AND OTHER INTERLACED PATTERNS.

a larger band having four closed loops. The effect would probably be improved by turning the design through 45 degrees; it would then appear as a kind of interlaced cross.

I. From a Slab at Fuerty. ($6\frac{1}{2}$ in. diameter.)

A simple knot consisting of two figure-of-eight bands interlaced and arranged to fill a semicircular panel.

---

[6] Compare also F, Plate xiii.

CHAPTER VI.

FRET PATTERNS[1]

NEXT to be considered are the fret patterns so freely used in Celtic decoration; they are apparently derived from the ancient Greek fret border or " Walls of Troy " pattern, which is itself seen on some of the earlier slabs at Clonmacnois, and on crosses such as those at Ferns and Monasterboice. When the Celts became acquainted with it they appear to have quickly developed it in many ways; such as placing it diagonally, expanding it sideways to fill broad panels, and altering the position and number of the bends.

The elementary form of the fret is a continuous line or band lying straight between certain points at which it is sharply bent in such a manner that no part crosses another. The only exception to this straightness, apart from careless workmanship, is that when the boundary of the panel is curved, adjacent parts of the design may be curved in sympathy. The angle of bending is usually 90 or 45 degrees, but occasionally a different effect is obtained or a panel of special proportions filled by altering the number of degrees.

It is evident that a line may be bent several times in the same direction, giving in combination the *key-pattern*, or alternately in opposite directions, which produces the *step-pattern*. Those designs in which the band is bent twice in one direction and then twice in the other may perhaps be looked on as an intermediate form.

In the majority of fret patterns the lines are placed diagonally in the panel as in this position they contrast better with the boundaries and produce a richer effect. Mr. Romilly Allen suggests that this may have arisen from the custom of setting out interlacing on a diagonal network which could as easily be utilized for frets. Vertical, horizontal and diagonal bars are used together in many cases, and this practice of employing bars lying in more than two directions is very characteristic of the Celtic use of fret patterns.

Frets and spirals are often joined in one design; of this several examples are illustrated. The two styles unite easily, and the contrast of angles and curves improves the appearance and adds to the variety of

---

[1] Not to be confused with the *Heraldic* use of the word

the patterns, see for instance J, Figure 7. Though many effective borders and some fine panels exist, fret patterns do not on the whole occupy so prominent a place or take such a number of intricate forms on Irish monuments as they do on those of Scotland.[2]

PLATES XXVII. AND XXVIII.

No. 56. From Dysert O'Dea Cross. (15½ in. × 8 in.)
A square key-pattern. It is not often used except in the form of the classic border (A, Figure 7), of which this design is a variety expanded laterally to cover a broad surface.

No. 57. From the North Cross, Ahenny. (14¾ in. × 12¾ in.)
A simplified form of square fret which perhaps belongs more to the step than the key patterns. Immediately above it on the stone is carved the Zoömorphic spiral design shown at B, Figure 11; and the stiff rectangular lines of this fret were probably intended to emphasise by contrast the flowing curves of the adjoining spirals.

No. 58. From the South Cross, Ferns. (About 16 in. wide.)
A good example of the ordinary diagonal key-pattern, it is similar to No. 56, but turned so that the lines point towards the angles of the panel. This is a commoner variety of Celtic fret, and one which, by the turning of the marginal lines parallel to the sides, introduces the characteristic feature of lines placed in more than two directions.

No. 59. From Dysert O'Dea Cross. (15½ in. × 8 in.)
A diagonal fret like the last, but having a different effect because the angles between the sets of lines are slightly varied from 90 degrees, so that some are acute and others obtuse. This modification may originally have been suggested by panels whose proportions did not suit the rectangular fret.

No. 60. From the South Cross, Castledermot. (15½ in. × 10 in.)
A panel of diagonal fret in which vertical lines are introduced in the centre as well as at the sides. It practically resolves itself into two borders of triangular key-pattern placed together symmetrically.

No. 61. From Killamery Cross. (16¼ in. × 11½ in.)
A very characteristic example of Celtic fret in which vertical as well as diagonal lines are present all through the design. An identical pattern is found on the cross of Kilree in the same district, and various modifications may be noticed in the *Book of Kells* and other manuscripts.

No. 62. From the North Cross, Ahenny. (13 in. × 13 in.)
This fine pattern is shown on a somewhat larger scale than the others on account of the closeness of the design. It is another instance of diagonal key-pattern with vertical bars, and has in addition diamond-shaped openings showing the back-ground.
The sculptor has carefully avoided the rather monotonous appearance to which panels of fretwork are liable, by removing the centre and sub-

[2] Eight varieties are illustrated in *Celtic Art*, pp. 280, 282.

stituting an interlaced knot of simple but effective form. This plan of placing one design in the centre of another is uncommon except in the case of projecting bosses which often bear a pattern distinct from that which surrounds them; a design more strictly comparable to this one is carved on a shaft found at Gallen Priory, near Ferbane.[3] There the centre is an animal and the surrounding pattern a triangular fret.

The present fret is several times used in the illuminated Gospels, No. 51, in the St. Gall Library, and may be seen in the plates of that manuscript published in the *Ulster Journal of Archaeology* for 1860.

No. 63. From Muiredach's Cross, Monasterboice. (11 in. × 9¾ in.)
A fret with T-shaped keys and lines placed in four directions. The panel, which is on the base of the cross, contains two repetitions of the design.

No. 64. From the High Cross, Kilfenora. (11 in. × 11 in.)
Another arrangement of frets so placed in a square that the lines radiate in all directions from the centre. This pattern is symmetrical, but modifications are often used in which the keys follow each other in one direction swastika-fashion. An example is given at D, Figure 9.

No. 65. From an erect Slab at Ardane. (7½ in. × 1¾ in.)
A step border in which the lines occupy a diagonal position. This is not often seen on monuments of the early Christian period, though common in work of earlier and later date.

No. 66. From Slab No. 86 at Clonmacnois. (1¾ in. wide.)
A step border of simple form, common on metalwork and in manuscripts as well as on stone. In the *Book of Kells* it forms the border of the roof of the Temple, and also appears in other places.

PLATES XXIX. AND XXX.

No. 67. From Bealin Cross. (9¼ in. × 8¾ in.)
A simple and typical step pattern in which the steps are placed vertically and horizontally. These step patterns are not of frequent occurrence on Irish monuments but may be noticed filling small panels in the illuminated manuscripts.

The L-shaped bands in the corners recall the angle-pieces on some of the square panelled slabs at Clonmacnois.

No. 68. From Dysert O'Dea Cross. (26 in. × 19½ in.)
An effective step pattern of the same kind as the last mentioned, but arranged in a continuous or repeated form. It is curious that the centres of one of the side rows of lozenge-shaped figures are in relief while those of the other rows are sunk.

On the upper part of Killamery Cross there is a step pattern of similar but plainer character, made up of cross-shaped sinkings disposed in

---

[3] Illustrated in the *Journal of the Royal Society of Antiquaries of Ireland*, vol. xxxviii. (1908), p. 62.

vertical and horizontal rows.   The spaces between contain squares of the
same size as the arms of the crosses.   Patterns of this kind fill the background of several slabs at Inis Cealtra,[4] and are often found on metalwork.

No. 69.   From the North Cross, Ahenny.   (8¼ in. × 5 in.)
A step pattern in which the steps are placed diagonally in the panel.
The design is greatly worn but being a simple one it can be restored.
There are three repetitions side by side, portion of the repeat is illustrated to show how it introduces a new element; that of opposed chevrons
with straight lines between.
This pattern may be seen in the *Book of Kells*, for instance, on the
page containing the portrait of St. Mark or St. Luke, where it fills the
centres of the small squares over the attendant figures.

No. 70.   From the West Cross, Monasterboice.   (9¾ in. × 9¾ in.)
A fret which presents the feature of steps and keys combined in one
pattern.   The upper part of the design is curiously modified so as to bring
the highest line of steps horizontal instead of vertical like the others.
When intricate patterns are modified in this kind of way it often requires
close examination to distinguish just where the change comes in.

No. 71.   From Tihilly Cross.   (11 in. × 8 in.)
A design like the last, but having spirals substituted for some of the
steps.   By this device additional variety and contrast are obtained.   A
similar pattern is carved on the North Cross at Duleek.

No. 72.   From Dysert O'Dea Cross.   (15½ in. × 14½ in.)
A step pattern combined with interlacing, and having some of the
centres modified to a circular form.[5]   This union of fret and interlacing
is unsusal.   The same design is used (though without interlacing) in the
Royal M.S. 1 E. VI. in the British Museum, to decorate the bases of
the pillars enclosing the first words of St. Luke's Gospel.[6]

No. 73.   From Termonfechin Cross.   (15½ in. × 5 in.)
A very perfect example of key pattern with inserted spirals.   The
frets are slightly altered in two cases so as to have three bands rather
than four entering each spiral coil.

No. 74.   From the West Cross, Kells.   (16 in. × 8¾ in.)
This fret is similar to No. 58, but is varied and perhaps improved by
having the band doubled, and the ends of all the keys rounded into spirals
as well as slightly raised.

No. 75.   From the West Cross, Monasterboice.   (19 in. × 10 in.)
This is a panel of combined fret and spiral design.   The spirals cover
the surfaces of seven rounded bosses regularly arranged in the panel, and

---

[4] Illustrated in the *Proceedings of the Royal Irish Academy,* vol. xxxiii.,
Section C., Plates xxiii. and xxiv.
[5] The effect of this modification is to produce a central cross of the type seen
on tenth century slabs at Clonmacnois.
[6] Illustrated in Westwood's *Palaeographia sacra Pictoria,* Plate 14.

the frets occupy the intermediate spaces. The straight bands of the frets run unbroken into the curves of the spirals and form an effective design.

FIGURE 7.—FRET BORDERS.

A. From Slab No. 120 at Clonmacnois. (5¼ in. × 2½ in.)

The Greek fret, from which the other varieties have been developed, and which is in all probability founded on the *swastika*.

This design can be altered in many ways without losing its character, and several examples are carved on early slabs at Clonmacnois; it also forms part of the decoration of many crosses. In the present instance the incised portions are continuous and the raised lines are detached; evidently it could be varied by making the latter continuous, by changing the number of angles in each element, and by reversing the relief.

B. From Slab No. 268 at Clonmacnois. (8¼ in. × 2 in.)

Another form of Greek fret in which the element is T-shaped; in relief, and continuous. It, like the last mentioned, might be varied by breaking the continuity, altering the number of turns, and reversing the relief. In its non-continuous form it corresponds to the C-curve of the spiral designs, as the last example does to the S-curve.

C. From a Slab at Gallen Priory. (5½ in. × 2¼ in.)

A typical border of *triangular fret*, in which the lines are bent at angles of about 60 instead of 90 degrees. This border has the ends of the elementary lines bent in opposite directions and so belongs to the S class: it was not often used and there seems to be no example of the C-form, which would give a kind of *cramp* pattern.

Panels like this border are carved on a cross-shaft at the same place and on the South Cross at Clonmacnois.

D. From the larger cross at Ardane. (9 in. × 3 in.)

Part of a circular step border, the detached portions of which are in relief. It will be seen that this is a Greek fret reduced to its simplest shape; it is used in the *Book of Kells* and on metalwork, and has also been found on Pre-Christian monuments.

E. From the South Cross, Ahenny. (9 in. × 3½ in.)

A double zigzag or meander pattern from the under side of the ring; the central line representing an obtuse angle on the stone. These zigzags are really Greek frets simplified and placed diagonally. Ornament of this kind is used to fill long narrow spaces in some of the initial letters in the *Book of Durrow;* for example, those heading the Gospels of St. Mark and St. Luke.

F. From the North Cross, Ahenny. (11½ in. × 2¾ in.)

A key pattern of simple form which fills the segments of the ring. The space is divided into square compartments, in each of which is a pair of diagonal L-shaped keys springing from opposite angles and connected to the remaining angles by extra bars.

G. From Muiredach's Cross, Monasterboice. (12 in. × 3½ in.)

A good though rather stiff fret border divided into squares like the last, but having each square filled by two T-shaped keys placed diagonally.

FIG. 7.—FRET BORDERS.

These figures are often used in the more complex patterns and often fill the angles when the rest of the design is quite different.

H. From the South Cross, Clonmacnois. (15½ in. × 3¼ in.)

A border in which the arms of the T-shaped figures are unsymmetrical and bent at angles of about 120 degrees, thus resembling triangular fretwork. Slab No. 81 at Clonmacnois exhibits a fine circular border of this type,[7] and it is also seen round circular panels in the *Book of Kells*. In metal it is used to decorate the robes of several figures on the Breac Moedoc.[8]

I. From the Market Cross, Kells.   (18 in. × 3¼ in.)
A closely worked fret having the sides occupied by figures like those of the last example, and the centre by detached portions of Greek fret placed diagonally.

J. From Muiredach's Cross, Monasterboice.   (19¾ in. × 3½ in.)
An effective design formed of elements resembling those of the last two patterns; but with the added features of central bars parallel to the sides, and spirals placed at intervals.

FIGURE 8.—CIRCULAR AND
SEMICIRCULAR FRET PATTERNS.

A. From a Slab at Inchagoil.   (About 8 in. diameter.)
A fret which shows how the straight lines near the boundary become curved in sympathy.   The correspondence between spirals and frets may be noticed by comparing this figure with B, Figure 3.

B. From the High Cross, Kilfenora.   (22½ in. diameter.)
A design of the same class as A but involving a greater number of bands.   Variations of this are carved on slabs at Clonmacnois, Fuerty, etc.

C. From a Slab at Clonfert.   (5½ in. diameter.)
A simple cruciform pattern of one band which combines fret and interlaced work.[9]

D. From Pillar Stone No. 2 at Glencar.[10]   (7 in. diameter.)
This circle is filled in with a pattern which divides it into three (or six) parts instead of the usual four.   It is placed under a cross and may have a symbolic meaning like those at J and K, Figure 9.

E. From a Slab at Glencolumbkille.   (About 16 in. diameter.)
Another fret pattern which divides the circle in the same way as D. Designs of this type are rare on stone, but are frequently employed in illumination; they divide the surface into a number of separate compartments, and the suggestion has been made that they have been adapted from Cloisonné enamels.

F. From Slab No. 156 at Clonmacnois.   (7¾ in. × 4½ in.)
A symmetrical fret of T-shaped elements arranged to fill a panel containing rather more than a semicircle.

---

[7] Illustrated at C, Plate xiv.
[8] Illustrated in *Archaeologia*, vol. xliii., p. 140.
[9] For the complete slab, see Plate xiii., E.
[10] Illustrated in the *Transactions of the Royal Irish Academy*, vol. xxvii., p. 44.

G. From the same Slab as F. (7¾ in. × 4½ in.)

An unsymmetrical fret, the centre of which has been altered to a spiral form. Several instances of this process are illustrated elsewhere.

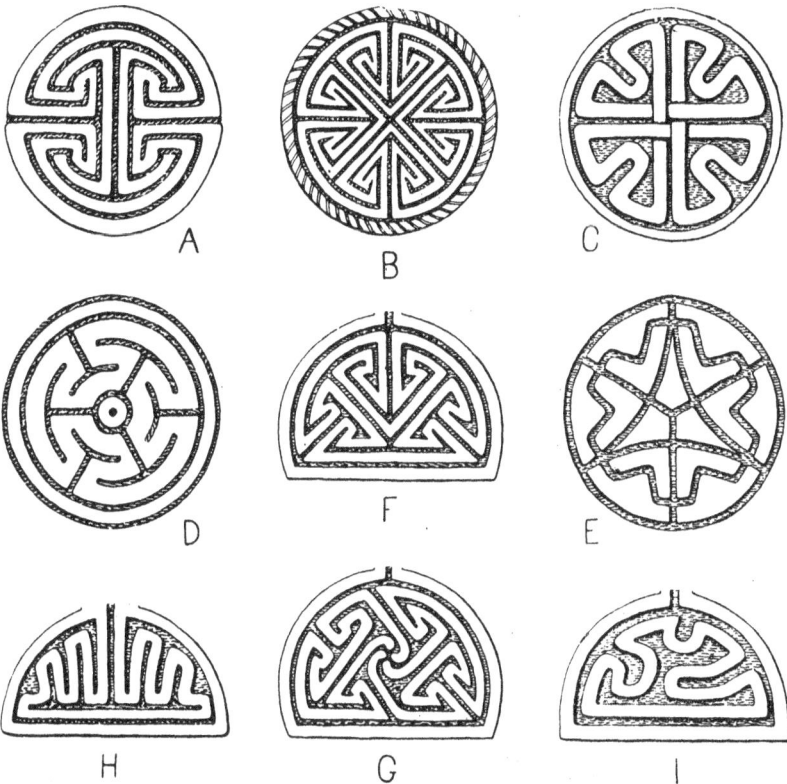

FIG. 8.—CIRCULAR AND SEMICIRCULAR FRET PATTERNS.

H. From a Slab at Clonfert. (7½ in. × 4 in.)

This is from the same stone as C, and shows a fret of the zigzag or toothed form. This also is seldom seen on stone, but often in illuminated manuscripts.

I. From Slab No. 142 at Clonmacnois. (6¼ in. × 3¾ in.)

This is an unsymmetrical fret of one endless band, irregularly placed, but leaving no large space unfilled.

CHAPTER VII.

GEOMETRICAL SYMBOLS

EOMETRICAL or abstract designs were in some cases used as symbols as well as ornament, and may conveniently be illustrated here. In some cases the meaning is well known, in others it is doubtful. One example only of the Sacred Monogram, or rather of the transitional form between it and the cross, has been found in Ireland. This is a rude cross about 2 feet long, with expanded arms and a pointed foot, incised on a sepulchral slab in the townland of Coumduff, near Anascaul, Co. Kerry. The Monogram is suggested by a curve or spiral which springs from the sinister angle of the upper arm, and represents the loop of the P. The expanded lateral arms stand for the X.[1]

FIGURE 9.

A. From a Stone at Inismurray. (15½ in diameter).

A Greek cross surrounded by a circle. The cross is the chief symbol, and illustrations of its varieties would alone fill a volume; this example is given as typical; others will be found in the plates and figures. The arms of this cross end in triquetras and the quadrants are occupied by threefold spirals which may be looked on as *triskelia* or three-armed swastikas. Crosses are not only designed and carved separately, but are often indicated by leaving cruciform hollows or spaces between the strands of designs; of this C, Figure 6, is a good example.

B. From Pillar Stone No. 2 at Glencar. (3 in. × 3 in.)

A swastika of ordinary form surrounded by a square frame with inwardly projecting lines. The swastika or fylfot, with its curved forms, is not infrequent on Irish monuments; it is a very ancient device and is found all through Europe and Asia. As used on Christian monuments it is thought to be simply a variety of cross.[2]

---

[1] Illustrated in the *Kerry Archaeological Magazine*, vol. i. (1912), p. 479 and in the *Journal R.S.A.I.*, vol. l. (1920), p. 65.

[2] *The Reliquary*, vol. xxii. (1881), p. 1.

FIG. 9. —GEOMETRICAL DESIGNS AND LETTERS USED AS SYMBOLS.

The arms of swastikas may turn in either direction, and it is an interesting fact that in Tibet, where they are still in use for religious purposes, the opposite forms serve to mark the opposing sects.[3] In Ireland both kinds are found, and it seems to be the rule that swastikas on the same monument turn in the same direction. The instances are however few, and further discoveries may upset this idea.[4] An example of the opposite form to this one is given at C, Plate XII.

C. From Slab No. 120 at Clonmacnois. (2⅛ in. × 1⅞ in.)

A swastika of the type sometimes known as *Chinese;* having a second turn to each arm. Another example, from Killamery Cross, is illustrated in No. 27, Plates XIX. and XX.

When swastikas of this kind are arranged in diagonal rows to produce a continuous pattern, the spaces between take the shape of crosses. This is well seen on the back of the Shrine of St. Patrick's Bell, where the crosses are openings in a metal plate, and the swastikas are the bars between them. Swastikas of this form are repeated many times side by side on the base of the Ardagh Chalice.

D. From the South Cross, Ahenny. (5¼ in. × 5 in.)

An ornamental form of swastika in which the lines are doubled, placed diagonally, and turned several times in the same direction at acute angles.

E. From Pillar Stone No. 1 at Glencar. (3 in. × 3 in.)

A case in which the arms are curved and placed in a frame shaped to match. It seems to stand between the angular type and those of spiral form which follow.

F. From a Slab at Inisbofinne. (4¼ in. diameter.)

A curved swastika or *tetraskelion*, like those on many slabs at Clonmacnois. The only difference is that here the radiating grooves stop short of the surrounding circle, a peculiarity which indicates that the hollows and not the intervening ridges are the important part.[5]

G. From Slab No. 154 at Clonmacnois. (4½ in. diameter.)

A design like the last, but having three arms only; it closely resembles the centres of many spiral patterns. As well as being plain like this one, *Triskelia* are occasionally carved in Zoömorphic form; an instance appears in No. 54 where three birds radiating from a centre are carved at either side of the cross. At Clonmacnois one of the circular plaques on the principal cross exhibits three dolphins similarly placed.

H. From Killamery Cross. (12 in. diameter.)

A triskelion consisting of three loops. The stone is rather worn and indistinct, but on a close examination there is no doubt as to the design.

---

[3] Sven Hedin, *Trans Himalaya*, p. 404.

[4] Four swastikas of this form appear on the cross-bearing page, which faces St. John's Gospel in the *Book of Lindisfarne*, two turn in one direction and two in the other.

[5] For a good account of the swastika, see Sir E. Ray Lankester, *Secrets of Earth and Sea*, p. 191.

I. From the S.E. Cross, Rhefert, Glendalough. (4¼ in. diameter.)

A design of the same kind as G, but having two divisions or arms instead of three; it fills the centre of a circular cross panel. The resulting figure is very similar to the symbol called "Tomoye" in Japan and the East, where it denotes triumph or success. Sir E. Ray Lankester suggests that it may be the origin of the swastika, two curved lines being crossed as at F.[6]

J. From a Pillar-Stone at Caherlehillan. (6 in. diameter.)

The stone bears a cross with spiral ends, below which is the figure shown. The circle being a line without beginning or end was used as a symbol of eternity; when placed under a cross as in this case it may denote the world overcome.[7] A circle surrounding a cross as at A may also be symbolic. Compare also D and E, Figure 8, which are placed below crosses, but are joined to them unlike this example and K, which are separate. A plain circle unaccompanied by any other figure is cut on an ogam pillar at Drumlusk, near Kenmare.

K. From Slab No. 190 at Clonmacnois. (4½ in. diameter.)

A circle placed below a cross and containing a fret pattern. The stone is in bad condition, but the design can be recovered except that it is uncertain how far the fret was modified where it comes in contact with the circle. The spaces between the I-shaped figures form swastikas, but arranged in a different manner from those mentioned in connection with C.

L. From Donaghmore Cross, Co. Tyrone. (About 5 in. × 4 in.)

A triquetra formed of two parallel bands. The triquetra being a three-pointed knot without beginning or end is usually thought to symbolise the Trinity, though some authorities doubt this. It is one of the most frequently used designs, and instances may be noticed amongst the panels illustrated.

M. From Slab No. 162 at Clonmacnois. (5¾ in. × 5¼ in.)

A triquetra of one band only; it is an unusually well cut and perfect design.

N. From the same Slab as M. (5¾ in. × 5¼ in.)

This is a design which corresponds to the triquetra, one being a *fret* and the other an *interlaced* pattern. It occupies the arm of the cross opposite to that containing M, and may also be symbolic.

The part of the slab on which it appeared has unfortunately been lost, but the design is preserved in Petrie's drawing.[8]

O. From a Slab at Church Island, Waterville.

The symbolic letters *alpha* and *omega*. They are drawn from a rubbing, as are the following.

P. From a Slab at St. Kevin's, Glendalough.

The same letters, carved in a slightly different form.

---

[6] *Secrets of Earth and Sea,* p. 210.

[7] F. E. Hulme, *Symbolism in Christian Art,* p. 49.

[8] *Round Towers and Ecclesiastical Architecture of Ireland,* p. 325.

CHAPTER VIII.

ZOÖMORPHIC DESIGNS

OMPARISON of the foregoing linear designs with those based on animal forms, makes it clear that any of the former can be rendered Zoömorphic by modifying the terminal portions so as to represent the heads, feet, and tails of animals. This is frequently done to spirals and interlacements; frets are not so treated on early monuments, though something of the kind may be seen in Romanesque architecture, where zigzag or chevron mouldings often end in animal heads.

Designs thus treated form a connecting link between the purely abstract and the completely Zoömorphic classes. The true Zoömorphic type consists entirely of the bodies, limbs, and other appendages of men and animals, and is more suited to interlaced than to spiral or other patterns. The latter usually belong to the intermediate class; A and B, Figure 11, are examples, and others are given in the Plates; while C, Figure 11, is a completely Zoömorphic spiral. Interlaced animal patterns, on the other hand, are most often completely Zoömorphic, as shown at A and B, Figure 12; C in the same figure being a knotted pattern terminating in animal heads and tails.

Amongst the designs illustrated in the plates are human figures with the hair, beards and limbs interlaced, and animals with tongues, tails, ears, crests and legs similarly treated. It has been asserted that the human and animal figures are always furnished with the proper number of limbs, &c.; but this does not hold good in every case unless one limb or ear may be supposed hidden behind the other. Thus in No. 95 (also shown in the frontispiece) the figures have, to all appearance, one leg and one arm each; and in No. 91 the curious animals in the centre show two forelegs and one hindleg. If it were not for the latter they might almost be taken for birds.

Animals are nearly always represented in profile and occasionally have the head turned to show the full face. Very rarely a dorsal view is given; see No. 96 and Figures 11 and 12. On the Cross of Drumcliff frogs are carved in this position in high relief. Any suitable number of animals may be carved in a panel, two or four being most frequent, and they may be placed in various positions such as face to face, back to back, with bodies crossed, or following each other in the same direction. Sometimes, in addition to having their limbs interlocked, they are interlaced with and bound round by serpents.

PLATES XXXI. AND XXXII.

No. 76. From Termonfechin Cross. (18 in. × 7 in.)

This is a typical example of freely drawn spirals rendered Zoömorphic by the insertion of animal heads at the angles. Two spirals would naturally interlock at each of these points, but instead of this, one spiral ends in a head from the tongue of which the other proceeds. This design occupies the lower part of one side of the shaft and, like those on the other sides, is in such good preservation as to suggest that the stone must have been partially buried for a long time. Above it, but much worn, is a panel with more flowing spirals and two human heads worked into the centre.

No. 77. From the North Cross, Ahenny. (18 in. × 13 in.)

A handsome spiral design the expanded parts of which are unusually elaborate. The central coil consists of four spirals united in pairs and having curved filling pieces between. The outer spirals end in conventional birds' heads, claws, &c., thus resembling the designs on the back of the ring of the Tara Brooch, though the latter are even more conventionalised. Another design of this kind is given at B, Figure 11.

No. 78. From the West Cross, Kells. (12¼ in. × 9 in.)

A panel of eight serpents, partly spiral and partly interlaced. The heads are in pairs, one biting the other, the dorsal aspect being shown. The tails of the four central serpents are coiled in one direction so as to suggest a curved swastika. One angle of the design is unfortunately broken, but is shown restored in Plate XXXII.

No. 79. From Bealin Cross. (15 in. × 8½ in.).

This panel is filled by a serpent continuously looped on itself. The head is crested and bites the first loop; the tail is broad and fish-like and has three points. A similar design, much injured, is carved on a cross-shaft now standing in Temple Dowling at Clonmacnois.

No. 80. From the North Cross, Duleek. (6¼ in. × 5¼ in.)

A serpent with large erect head and curiously plaited tail; it has also a very peculiar twist in the centre of the thick coil. This figure may, perhaps, have had a symbolic meaning; though animal designs of the latter kind are in most cases natural representations, interlacing being reserved for decorative panels.

No. 81. From the Market Cross, Kells. (11¼ in. × 9 in.)

Four serpents wreathed round two bosses which are ornamented with combined spiral and fret patterns. The sides are filled in by triangular interlaced designs.

No. 82. From the North Cross, Duleek. (9¼ in. × 5 in.)

Two serpents or sea-horses represented in plan, with ears and fish-like tails. They are interlaced in such a way that one forms the upper and the other the lower knot. In the corresponding panel on the opposite side of the cross there are two animals of the same kind interlaced in a six-cord plait.

No. 83.   From Muiredach's Cross, Monasterboice.   (20 in. × 6 in.)

A striking design which from its position on the under side of the ring is in unusually good preservation.   It represents two serpent-like animals twisted together: the heads have large eyes and ears, the tails are square in shape, and the bodies are ornamented with longitudinal lines and rows of pellets.   Three human heads, well carved, fill the centres of the twists; they are clean-shaven and have the hair arranged in loose curls. (See also No. 97, Plates XXXV. and XXXVI., which shows one of these heads on a larger scale.)   Similar designs occupy corresponding places on crosses at Clonmacnois and Durrow Abbey, but as these monuments are smaller the ornament is somewhat simplified.   At the former place there are only two twists; at the latter, instead of two animals, one only is shown twisted on itself.

No. 84.   From the North Cross, Duleek.   (9 in. × 5 in.)

Two animals interlaced, and placed with their heads at diagonally opposite corners of the panel.   They have nondescript or dog-like heads, attenuated bodies, and tails spirally coiled: one leg only is shown.   In this design the animals are placed in a reversed position to each other, and the neck and leg of each pass through the coil formed by the body of the other.   These animals are of a type which lends itself readily to interlaced work and is frequently used.   At B, C, D, Figure 10, it is seen adapted to borders and at A, Figure 12, four such animals are arranged to fill a square panel.

PLATES XXXIII. AND XXXIV.

No. 85.   From the North Cross, Duleek.   (6¼ in. × 5 in.)

A solitary animal of dog-like appearance, having its legs and tail interlaced, one foreleg only being shown.   Such designs usually have two or more animals interlaced or bound round with serpent forms; a single one is rare.

No. 86.   From Drumcliff Cross.   (19 in. × 5¼ in.)

A long narrow panel with an effective design of two crested dragons whose bodies are crossed, this being the position most frequently adopted in ornament of the kind.   The tails and two of the forelegs are joined together though there does not seem to be any reason for this, and the design would look better if they terminated separately.   The panel is placed upright on the stone, but was evidently intended for the horizontal position it occupies in the plates.

No. 87.   From Tihilly Cross.   (11 in. × 4¼ in.)

This is an example of the Zoömorphic panels made from designs originally intended to form borders by repetition.   One element of the border is here taken and more or less satisfactorily provided with ends. The end towards which the heads point is well managed; the other less so as it is too crowded.   It would, perhaps, have been better to have left out the last head, and filled the space with the tail and leg of the animal next to it.   The design is in wonderful preservation except that a lower angle is chipped away; the restoration of this part shown in Plate XXXIV. is conjectural. The spiral ears and the wrinkles on necks and paws may be noted, as in most carvings these details are worn away.

No. 88. From Kinnitty Cross. (9½ in. × 7½ in.)
Two birds facing each other; they are furnished with crests and their necks and legs are interlaced. They have also spirals carved on their bodies at the junction of the wings: a device often used in early work to represent hair, feathers, or folds of skin. This design may have had a symbolic meaning; it is of interest, as birds are not very often represented on Irish monuments; and as it resembles the ornament on certain jewels of Mycenaean Age,[1] which exhibit birds in the same position but without the Celtic interlacings.

Count Goblet D'Alviella[2] is inclined to deduce the double-headed eagle of Russia, &c., from the fusing together of the birds in such designs. Compare with these the birds in Nos. 102 and 126.

No. 89. From Dysert O'Dea Cross. (19 in. × 10 in.)
A panel containing two dragons facing each other, and interlaced with two serpents, one of which has curious foot-like expansions where it crosses the bodies of the dragons. The latter have protruding tongues and collars or bands about their necks. There is some uncertainty as to the exact form of the interlacing near the middle of the right-hand side; one head and two tails are grouped there, and it seems as though part of one band may have been omitted.

No. 90. From Dysert O'Dea Cross. (14 in. × 9 in.)
Two dragons placed back to back and each interlaced with the tongue and tail of the other; as well as with two serpents, one of which has two bodies uniting in a single head.

No. 91. From Bealin Cross. (46 in. × 12 in.)
A large and remarkable design consisting of three greatly elongated animals with bird-like heads, but showing one foreleg and two hindlegs. The neck and foreleg of each is interlaced with the coiled body of the next; the uppermost being completed by having its neck and foreleg bent back into a horizontal position.

One only of the three animals is provided with a tail, though the others might just as well have had them, *and their omission throws the interlacing wrong.*[3] There is, of course, no neck or leg to pass through the lowest coil, but the vacancy is filled by the tail of a different animal placed at the bottom of the panel. This animal is heavy and thickset, and has apparently a human leg in its mouth (this may perhaps be intended for a tongue, but a leg is often thus represented), and its long drawn-out tail divides at the end into five leaf-shaped branches which may be intended to represent hair. At first sight the tail would, in fact, be taken for a palm tree like that at Ahenny (No. 126, Plates XLI. and XLII.); but two animals of the same kind and having similar tails are carved on

---

[1] Schuchhardt, *Schliemann's Excavations* (English Edition), p. 262.
[2] *The Migration of Symbols* (English Edition), p. 25.
[3] See description of B, Figure 10.

a fragment at Clonmacnois,[4] so that this example does not stand alone. The upper part of the design is repeated on a cross-shaft now in Temple Dowling at Clonmacnois,[5] and in the *Book of Kells* a pattern of this kind forms the border to the portrait of St. Mark or St. Luke, and appears with modifications on several other pages.

No. 92. From the North Cross, Ahenny. (13 in. × 13 in.)

A square panel of four men placed symmetrically with regard to the centre, and interlaced in a bold and effective manner. This design is superior to most of its kind in having the panel well filled without any great distortion of the figures, and in showing distinctly the proper number of limbs. In the more elaborate example at Monasterboice (No. 95, Plates XXXV. and XXXVI., also Frontispiece) each figure is greatly distorted and has one arm and one leg only.

The idea of four human figures thus interlaced is an early and favourite one, and is seen at Kells, Tihilly, Clonmacnois, and Old Kilcullen. Mr. Romilly Allen has illustrated a Scottish example[6] in which the figures are arranged as a swastika, a form which is also indicated in the design B, Figure 12. It has been suggested that this close interlacing of human figures is intended to symbolize the brotherhood and interdependence of Mankind.

No. 93. From the Market Cross, Kells. (11 in. × 9 in.)

A design of four men which differs slightly from the last. As this panel is oblong, two of the figures are nearer to each other than the remaining pair, and have one leg each enlarged and hooked together. In metal, good examples of this class of design are found on the Lismore Crosier; they have been illustrated in O'Neill's *Fine Arts and Civilization of Ireland*.

PLATES XXXV. AND XXXVI.

No. 94. From Dysert O'Dea Cross. (27½ in. × 17½ in.)

Part of the shaft of Dysert Cross, showing two admirable Zoömorphic designs. The upper is particularly free in its lines, and shows four elongated animals plaited together so as to have a head at each angle. In addition, the animals are bound round and interlaced with four serpents. The latter have coiled tails and broad heads with large eyes, but do not show the usual ears. The upper part of the design extends to the edge of the stone and has been somewhat damaged, but not so much so as to prevent restoration.

The lower panel contains a more formal design; two dragon-like animals with bodies crossed, and showing one fore and one hind leg each. The legs, as well as the tails and crests, are interlaced symmetrically; the whole arrangement resembling the design from Drumcliff shown in No. 86.

---

[4] Illustrated in the *Proceedings of the Society of Antiquaries of Scotland*, vol. xxxi. (1896-7), p. 312.

[5] Same reference, p. 310.

[6] *Celtic Art*, p. 288.

No. 95. From Muiredach's Cross, Monasterboice. (21½ in. × 11½ in.)

An elaborate design of eight men interlaced in sets of four.[7] The figures are provided with one arm and one leg only, as there is literally no room for more; the others may be taken as hidden. In this panel the interlacing is carried almost as far as it could be; the bodies, the hair, the beards, and the limbs being all treated in this way. The bodies appear to be clothed in tight-fitting garments which have a row of pellets down the front: with these pellets may be compared those in No. 83, another panel from the same monument. Four of the figures grasp the hair of the others, and these, in turn, hold the beards of the former.

It will be noticed that the beards are carved partly as circular knots and partly as spirals; and that the details in general are arranged to fill the panel without leaving any portion of the background uncovered. It is rather a triumph that amongst all these complications there is no false interlacing. A smaller copy of this design is carved on the lower part of the " Cross of the Scriptures " at Clonmacnois, and panels containing one half of it may be seen at Kells and Tihilly.

No. 96. From Killamery Cross. (50 in. × 42 in.)

This design is given as an example of a Zoömorphic cruciform panel; and as the head of this cross is one of the best proportioned it is illustrated in full. The cross-shaped part is occupied by four serpents surrounding a central boss; their heads are in pairs at the sides, one biting the other, while their tails fill the upper and lower portions. In the upper part they form a kind of spiral, and in the lower a twisted and interlaced pattern.

Above the serpents is an animal placed so as to show a back or dorsal view, a position not often seen except in the case of serpents. In this instance the animal resembles a skin spread out more than anything else. The carving on the boss and ring is too much worn to be made out.

No. 97. From Muiredach's Cross, Monasterboice. (2¾ in. × 2¼ in.)

A well carved head, one of six on the under side of the ring. Three of these heads are shown on a small scale in No. 83 which also indicates their surroundings.

No. 98. From Durrow Abbey Cross. (3 in. × 2¼ in.)

One of the heads occupying similar positions to those at Monasterboice, and interesting to compare with No. 97.

FIGURE 10.—ZOÖMORPHIC BORDERS.

A. From Termonfechin Cross. (9½ in. × 1¼ in.)

A continuous spiral terminating in a beast's or serpent's head at either end. It may be compared with the *interlaced* pattern ending in a head and tail, which is shown at G, Figure 5. Both are abstract designs rendered Zoömorphic by suitable additions.

B. From the Market Cross, Kells. (16½ in. × 3½ in.)

A border composed of animals with coiled tails and extended tongues,

---

[7] The frontispiece shows this panel on a large scale.

their bodies showing but one leg each. The body and leg are in each case interlaced through the coil formed by the tail of the preceding animal, and the tongue through that of the animal in front of the latter. As the

FIG. 10.—ZOÖMORPHIC BORDERS.

tail finishes in the centre and the other members pass right through, the number of strands proceeding from the middle of the coil to the circumference is even, *and the interlacing is necessarily wrong*. This is an unusual occurrence, and is the more remarkable because it might easily have been corrected by lengthening the ears, and bringing them to the centre of the coil from the top. (Compare No. 91, Plates XXXIII. and XXXIV.)

This design is also carved on the Cross of Muiredach, where it is placed on the ring alternately with that shown in the next figure. As it there fills a narrower space one turn of the coil is omitted.

C. From Muiredach's Cross, Monasterboice. (21 in. × 3 in.)

A simpler pattern of the same kind as the last, in which the tongues are omitted and each tail looped once round the body and leg of the next animal. As the end of the tail is brought to the outside of the loop, the interlacing is correct.

Borders of animals following each other are not very common, but this figure and the last are good examples. There is in them no attempt to complete the ends, the drawings give the entire designs.

At Lorrha, in the North of Tipperary, one of the cross bases has a border of animals round it; they are rather worn but appear to be horses treated naturally, and placed in a row right round the stone.[8]

D. From the West Cross, Monasterboice. (21½ in. × 4¼ in.)

Another form of Zoömorphic border in which animals like those in the last figure are crossed in pairs and placed between circular bosses. The patterns on these bosses are common on monumental slabs, and taken in connection with the type of cross carved on the under side of the ring, show that the sculptor was well accustomed to the decoration of such slabs.

E. From Dysert O'Dea Cross. (20½ in. × 4 in.)

A long narrow design of two animals placed across each other with their ears, legs, and tails interlaced. The lower portion of the interlacing near each end is worn and several of the loops are uncertain; but there seems to be no other arrangement by which the strands can be made to agree with the clear part of the design.

F. From the Market Cross, Kells. (18 in. × 3¼ in.)

Four men with beards and limbs interlaced. It should be noticed that the feet placed together belong to men at opposite ends; this curious arrangement is caused by the number of strands chosen for the central plait, if there were two more or two less the feet of the men at the same end would have been brought together.

This design is carved on the under side of the ring, and corresponding to it on the opposite quadrant is a similar pattern having one man only at either end. Each has one leg extended and the other doubled up; the extended legs are hooked together in the centre of the design. A more elaborate design of this kind is carved on a cross-shaft now placed in Temple Dowling at Clonmacnois.

Such designs are perhaps long panels rather than borders since there is no repetition, but it is clear that if the space allowed they might be repeated, the parts being connected by interlacing the hair as is done in other cases.

---

[8] Illustrated in the *Journal of the Royal Society of Antiquaries of Ireland*, vol. xxxix. (1909), p. 128.

FIGURE 11.—SPIRAL ZOÖMORPHIC DESIGNS.

A. From Tybroughney Cross.   (19½ in. × 18½ in.)

A good example of Zoömorphic trumpet-pattern formed of closely coiled spirals arranged to fill a circular panel.   Six C-shaped curves with

FIG. 11.—SPIRAL ZOÖMORPHIC DESIGNS.

large and small extremities are equally spaced round the circumference and connected together.   Adjacent pairs of the large coils are also joined by S-curves which throw off branches to form the central coil.   These curves, therefore, have the form of *triskelia* very like those shown at A, Figure 9. The centres of the coils are identical in opposite pairs; those which occupy a nearly-horizontal position on the stone, end in pear-shaped bulbs and are sunk as shallow cups. The centres of the other coils consist of birds' heads in various positions and are not sunk. Similar heads are illustrated at B, and at No. 77.

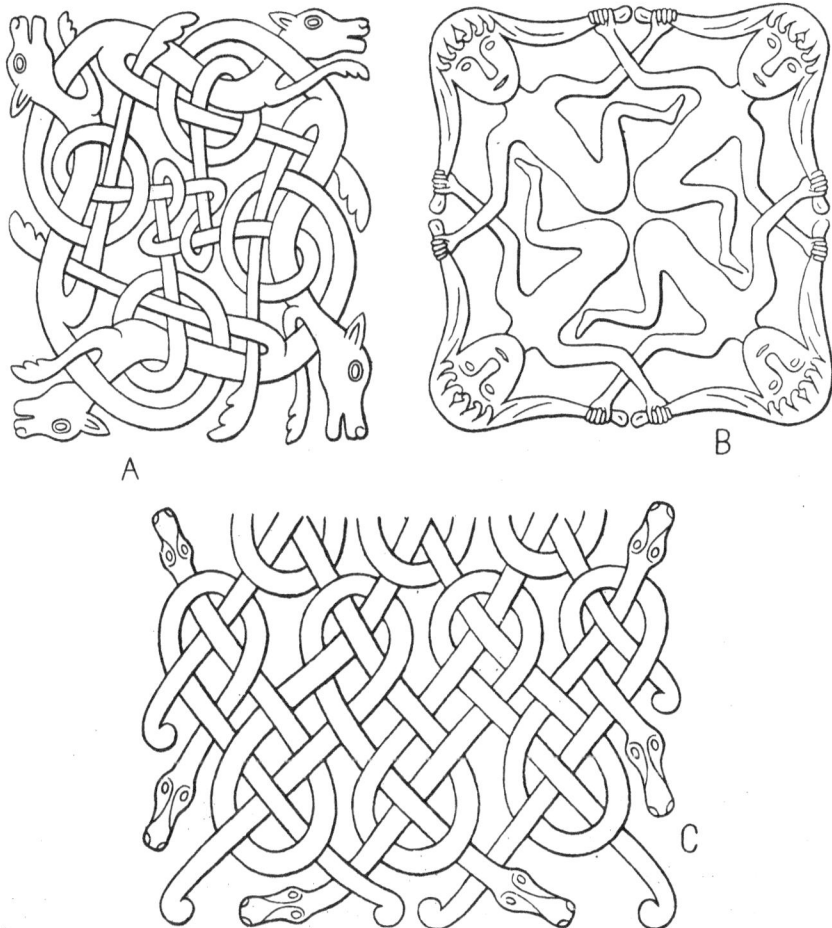

FIG. 12.—INTERLACED ZOÖMORPHIC DESIGNS.

This design greatly resembles that on a gold plate found at Mycenae,[9] but in the latter the spirals are imperfect and there is no divergence.

B. From the North Cross, Ahenny. (11½ in. × 11½ in.)

A panel of trumpet pattern in which the centre and angles are filled by spiral coils. The outer coils have Zoömorphic centres, and are all

[9] Illustrated in Schuchhardt's *Schliemann's Excavations*, p. 203 (English Edition), and reproduced in Coffey's *New Grange*, Figure 51, p. 66.

connected by S-curves; they are also joined to the central spiral by
C-curves which terminate in small separate coils inside the larger one.
The expanded portions of all the curves are admirably treated so as to
fill the available spaces.   It would be difficult to find a more effective
spiral design.

C. From Dromiskin Cross.   (18 in. × 18 in.)
Unlike **A** and **B** this is a completely Zoömorphic design, that is, it is
formed entirely of the bodies of animals, which are eight in number and
of the sea-horse or sea-serpent class.   Four of these are represented as
devouring the others; the tails of the former are coiled together in the
centre and slightly interlaced, while their crests form marginal coils
with the tails of the smaller animals.   This design is evidently a
Zoömorphic modification of the plain spiral pattern which has a centre
coil surrounded by eight others in a square.   (No. 3, Plates XV. and
XVI.)

FIGURE 12.—INTERLACED ZOÖMORPHIC DESIGNS.

A. From Kinnitty Cross.   (14 in. × 12 in.)
Four animals interlaced with their heads turned in one direction as a
swastika; the tails form each a single coil and are joined in adjacent pairs
after passing through the central knot.   On the title page this design is
shown adapted to a circular panel.

B. From the West Cross, Old Kilcullen.   (13 in. × 13 in.)
Four figures, apparently of children, arranged as a swastika, each
grasping the hair of the others.   The panel is in bad condition and the
outlines of the figures can alone be traced on the stone.   A more elaborate
design of the same type is carved on a cross-shaft now in Temple Dowling
at Clonmacnois.[10].
This design and the last are completely Zoömorphic, for those with
Zoömorphic *terminations*, see No. 79, G, Figure 5, and the following.

C. From the Market Cross, Glendalough.   (11 in. wide.)
Portion of a design consisting of figure-of-eight knots, furnished with
Zoömorphic finials in the form of serpent heads and tails.

---

[10] *Proceedings, Society of Antiquaries, Scotland,* vol. xxxi. (1896-7), p. 310.

A PANEL OF INTERLACED SERPENTS FROM DYSERT O'DEA CROSS.   (1/11.)

CHAPTER IX.

SYMBOLIC DESIGNS

EARLY Irish monuments are chiefly decorated with abstract ornament and pictorial subjects; symbolic figures being rather sparingly used. The geometrical symbols have been noticed in Chapter VII., and a number of animal and vegetable symbolic forms are collected in the plates which follow (XXXVII. to XLII.); other designs probably had meanings now lost.

Some of the emblems, such as the dove, the lamb, and the vine are clearly scriptural; others, like the stag, the griffin, and the manticora, are from the *Bestiary;* while others again are of traditional or doubtful origin. Although the curious symbols of unknown meaning found in Scotland are absent from Irish monuments, the latter present a sufficient puzzle in the remarkable design representing a human figure between two animals which seem to attack the head or ears. This subject is frequently repeated on monuments and buildings, as well as on metalwork[1] and manuscripts.[2]

Explanation is rendered difficult by the wide variation of the figures; the animals taking many forms and sometimes having human bodies. One of the photographs (No. 100) shows the central figure with horns, hoofs and a tail, and there is even a *sheela-na-gig* of this kind at Rath Church near Ennis.[3] These instances are sufficient to prove that the intention is not, as some have supposed, to represent Christ or Daniel.[4] The distinction between this subject and that of Daniel in the lion's den is further shown by their occurrence in adjoining panels on crosses at Castledermot and Moone Abbey.

---

[1] Three instances may be seen on the cumdach of the Stowe Missal, and one on the Killua shrine, both in the collection of the Royal Irish Academy. The former has been illustrated in the *Stowe Missal,* published by the Henry Bradshaw Society, and the latter in *The Antiquaries Journal,* vol. i. (1921), p. 48.

[2] See, for instance, D, Figure 13.

[3] This recalls the ancient πότνια θηρῶν, a nature deity supported by two animals. See also Evans in the *Journal of Hellenic Studies,* vol. xxi., p. 165.

[4] In early Christian art St. Menas was usually represented between two camels with heads turned downwards; but the Irish figures are not of this type, the animals being upright and aggressive. At Tréves an early tombstone, found in the Church of St. Maximin, has upon it two doves supporting between them the sacred monogram, represented in wheel form.

The marked similarity of this design to many found in ancient art is very noticeable and should not be overlooked. Several examples of the latter are illustrated for comparison in Figure 13 :—

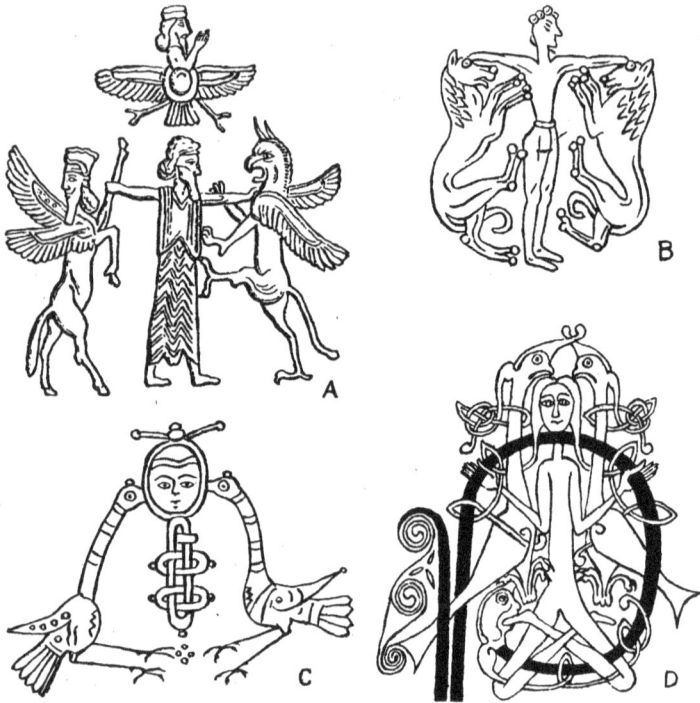

FIG. 13.—ANCIENT DESIGNS, SHOWING AN ANTHROPOMORPHIC FIGURE
BETWEEN TWO ANIMALS.

(For comparison with Nos. 99 to 102.)

A. From a seal found in Babylonia. See Layard, *Nineveh and Babylon*, p. 606.

B. From a Cretan gem. See Evans in the *Journal of Helenic Studies*, vol. xxi. (1901), p. 163.

C. From a Syriac Codex. (B. Museum, No. 7183.) See Westwood, *Palaeographia Sacra Pictoria*, Plate 6.

D. From an Irish Manuscript (No. 904 in the library of St. Gall, Switzerland). See Dr. Reeves in *The Ulster Journal of Archaeology*, vol. viii. (1860), p. 305.

The design of a tree between two animals seen in Nos. 121, 122 is closely related, and also resembles subjects found in ancient art, as well as on Norman architecture in England.[5] It is probably an older and

[5] A fine example of this period is carved on the ivory " horn " of Ulphus at York Minster. See *Vetusta Monumenta*, vol. i., and the *Archaeological Journal*, vol. xxvi., p. 1.

simpler variety, the tree (or pillar) symbolising the divinity afterwards represented in human form. Compare Figure 14:—

A. From an Assyrian bas-relief.[6] See Layard, *Nineveh and its remains*, vol. ii., p. 295.

B. From a Mycenaean gem. See Evans in *The Journal of Helenic Studies*, vol. xxi. (1901), p. 556.

C. From a Greek carving found at Priene. See Newton in *Antiquities of Ionia*, part iv., plate xxi.

FIG. 14.—ANCIENT DESIGNS, SHOWING A TREE BETWEEN TWO ANIMALS. (For comparison with Nos. 101, 102.)

Animal symbolism is rarely found on early slabs and pillars; most of the examples given are from carved crosses, but amongst them are a fish and a worm from slabs at Fuerty and Clonmacnois. Another instance which may be mentioned is that of a bird, probably a phoenix, placed over a cross on an erect slab at Caherlehillan in Kerry. Lower down on the same stone are what appear to be serpents.[7] Human heads are carved on two rough pillar stones at Carndonough, footprints on a slab at Inis Cealtra in Clare,[8] and the bust of a man on a pillar at Killeen Cormac in Kildare.[9]

---

[6] For an Assyrian example in metal work, see Layard, *Nineveh and Babylon*, p. 200. It greatly resembles C, Figure 14, and illustrates the connection between Assyrian and Ionian art. A Hittite example is illustrated in the *British Museum Report* on Carchemish, part i., plate B, 13, and an early Egyptian design (a palm tree between two giraffes) in the *Proceedings, Society of Biblical Archaeology*, vol. xxvi., p. 262.

[7] This stone is illustrated in plate xii.

[8] Illustrated in the *Proceedings of the Royal Irish Academy*, vol. xxxiii., Sect. C., plate xx., and in the *Journal of the Royal Society of Antiquaries of Ireland*, vol. xxxvi., p. 304, and reproduced in Fig. 15.

[9] Illustrated in the *Journal* last mentioned, vol. xii. (1873), p. 546.

Some or all of the scripture scenes depicted on the monuments have a secondary symbolic meaning, but as primarily representing historical events they are illustrated with the other pictorial carvings.

PLATES XXXVII. and XXXVIII.

No. 99.   From Dysert O'Dea Cross.   (19 in. × 9 in.)

A Zoömorphic design like Nos. 89 and 90, but having a human head placed between those of the dragons, so as to add whatever significance this frequently repeated device may have.   A design of the same type as this is repeated twice in a panel on the West Cross at Kells.   There, a human head is surrounded by serpents treated spirally, and the head of a serpent is brought close to it on either side.   Nos. 100 and 101 are varieties of the same idea, as is the figure in No. 54.

No. 100.   From the Market Cross, Kells.   (13 in. × 9½ in.)

This interesting panel shows a partially human figure between two wolf-like animals.   The central figure is furnished with horns, hoofs, and a tail, as well as a long plaited beard and moustache.

With this design may be compared the ancient Cretan gem shown at B, Figure 13; and others which have been described by Mr. Evans as bearing a *Daemon between two lions.*[10]

No. 101.   From Moone Abbey Cross.   (38 in. × 25 in.)

This is a portion of the base carved in two panels.   The lower contains a design of the same kind as the last mentioned; the three figures are human except that the outer ones have the heads of a goat and a cock. The central figure seems to push them away, and like all the figures on this cross is extremely short and square.   .

In the upper panel are two men seated on chairs or thrones, the backs of which end in animal heads; a bird hovers above and the figures hold between them a circular object.   Almost identical panels may be seen on the South Cross at Castledermot in the same district.   They have been illustrated by Mr. Romilly Allen in *Early Christian Symbolism of Great Britain and Ireland;* where additional examples of the figures and circular object will also be found.

A suggestion has been made that the latter design symbolises the Trinity and another that it represents the meeting of Abraham and Melchizedek; but the meaning is almost certainly fixed by the circumstance that on the Ruthwell Cross a similar scene is entitled in Latin " St. Paul and St. Anthony broke bread in the desert."   It should, therefore, be considered with the pictorial designs in Plate XLII., but is illustrated here to suit the available space.

No. 102.   From Tihilly Cross.   (8 in. × 4¾ in.)

Two birds with entwined necks, and having a human head placed between them at the base of the panel.   This is evidently another expression of the idea in the last three examples.

---

[10] *Journal of Hellenic Studies*, vol. xxi., p. 168.

A somewhat similar panel of two birds and a head is carved on the east window of the Priory Church at Glendalough: in it the head occupies the more usual position, being placed between the birds' beaks.

Another instance that may be mentioned is at Papil in the Shetland Islands; in it the animals are composite, having the feet and beaks of birds joined to human bodies.[11]

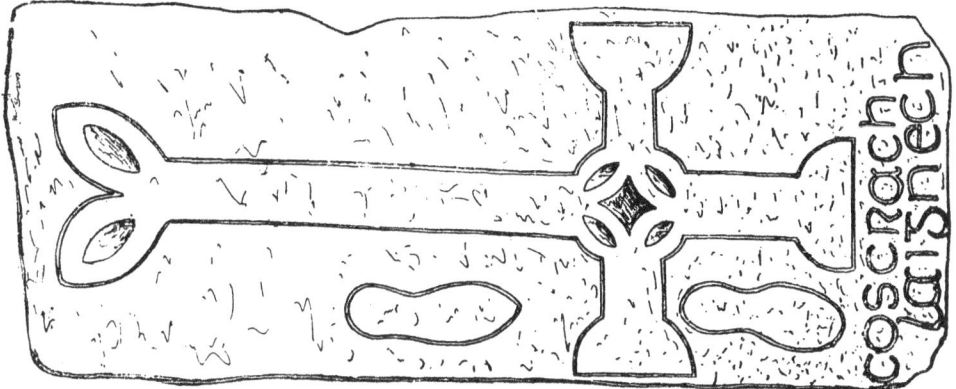

FIG. 15.—A TENTH CENTURY SLAB WITH SYMBOLIC FOOTPRINTS, AT INIS CEALTRA, CO. CLARE.

No. 103. From Muiredach's Cross, Monasterboice. (12½ in. diameter.)

The Dextera Dei, an emblem of the Creator. The hand and the decorated nimbus surrounding it are in unusually good preservation as they are carved on the under side of one arm of the cross. A smaller copy is carved in the same position on the "Cross of the Scriptures " at Clonmacnois. This position of the hand seems to suggest a similar idea to that indicated in medieval representations of the Trinity, where the Creator is seated and supports a crucifix by one or both hands placed beneath the arms of the cross. A third example of the hand, differing in form, appears as part of a scene carved on the Market Cross of Kells; it is illustrated in No. 129.[12]

The hand was also a Pre-Christian symbol of wide distribution; amongst the Romans it was commonly used as a household amulet and as a finial to military standards. It was known to the Phoenicians and Hebrews, amongst whom it denoted power, success, or victory.[13] These ancient examples usually have the fingers upwards, while as a Christian symbol it is most often represented as pointing downwards from heaven or from the clouds.

---

[11] Illustrated in *Early Christian Symbolism of Great Britain and Ireland*, p. 375.

[12] See also F. J. Bigger, *Proceedings, R.I.A.*, vol. xxii. (1900), p. 79.

[13] F. T. Elworthy, *Horns of Honour and other studies in the By-ways of Archaeology*, chapters iii. and iv.

No. 104. From the Market Cross, Kells, (5½ in. diameter.)

The Agnus Dei, emblematic of the Second Person of the Trinity. It is carved in a circular panel above the Crucifixion; a similar design is carved on the cross at Durrow Abbey. These early examples show the Lamb without the cross or banner afterwards added.

No. 105. From the "Cross of the Scriptures." Clonmacnois. (6 in. diam.)

A dove, the symbol of the Third Person of the Trinity. This circular panel or plaque is the lowest of the four which ornament the ring; and is thus placed below the Crucifixion and above a carving which appears to represent the Ecce Homo.

No. 106. From the North Cross, Duleek. (7 in. × 4¾ in.)

A winged lion holding up a book—the symbol of St. Mark. The eagle of St. John occupies the corresponding place on the opposite side of the cross, and is shown below. This is the only instance in which the symbols of the Evangelists have been noticed on an Irish monument,[14] and only two now exist at Duleek. The cap stone of the cross is, however, missing, and it is very probable that the symbols of St. Matthew and St. Luke were carved on the gable ends. They would then be immediately over those of St. Mark and St. John.

In this connection it is worthy of note that on the bell-shrine of Conal Cael, now in the British Museum, two of the evangelistic symbols are placed on the triangular ends of the roof or cap.

No. 107. From the North Cross, Duleek. (7 in. × 4¼ in.)

An eagle holding a book; the emblem of St. John. An eagle with a book between his claws is placed behind the figure of St. John in *The Book of Lindisfarne* and is found, with the other evangelistic symbols, in almost every copy of the Gospels illuminated in Celtic style. The scarcity on stone of these symbols is therefore very remarkable.

No. 108. From Muiredach's Cross, Monasterboice. (16 in. × 11½ in.)

An example of the symbolic vine, one of the few vegetable forms found on early monuments. *Such forms were never used as ornament*, but were introduced for the sake of the symbolism or as adjuncts to historical scenes. The sculptors seem to have taken no pleasure in representing vegetable forms, and in the case of the vine either, as here, introduced birds and squirrels amongst the branches,[15] or else, as in No. 111, reduced the tree to a kind of spiral or interlaced pattern. The root of the vine, it will be noticed, is here treated as a spiral.

Similar designs may be seen at Kells and Clonmacnois, and in metal-work on the head of a silver-plated crozier deposited in the National Museum by the Board of Trinity College.

No. 109. From a cross-slab at Fuerty. (7½ in. × 4 in.)

The only carving in Ireland of the fish, the earliest symbol of Christ. This arose as an anagram on the Greek letters I. X. Θ. Υ. Σ., the initials of the words forming the first confession of faith.[16]

[14] They are also carved on a cross at Ilkley, in Yorkshire.
[15] Perhaps suggested by the text, Canticles ii., 15.
[16] The fish was also an early symbol of baptism.

There are examples of this emblem in the *Book of Kells* and other manuscripts, but the fish carved on monuments have other meanings. See Nos. 112 and 120.

No. 110. From Slab No. 195 at Clonmacnois. (8 in. × 4 in.)
This and the preceding illustration are amongst the few animal forms found on early cross-slabs. The stone has at each corner a worm or serpent which seems to attack the angle of the cross, and is no doubt intended as an emblem of Death or of the Evil One.

PLATES XXXIX. AND XL.

No. 111. From the North Cross, Duleek. (9 in. × 8½ in.)
A representation of the vine which differs from the usual type, in being without the birds and animals often placed amongst the branches. In this design the tree has been reduced to an abstract pattern; the branching form and bunches of grapes alone indicating the vine.

A similar panel exists on the cross at Old Kilcullen, but the stone is so rough and worn that the design would hardly be recognised without a previous knowledge of this specimen. Several examples in metal, which somewhat resemble this, are worked on the Cumdach of the " Stowe Missal " now in the library of the Royal Irish Academy.

No. 112. From Moone Abbey Cross. (26 in. × 19 in.)
The Loaves and Fishes : It is not clear why two eel-like creatures are added at the sides, unless it is to fill the space. The loaves and fishes are also carved on the bases of the crosses at Castledermot in the same district; but have, in addition, a figure with hands stretched out over them, and in one case a number of small figures to represent the multitude. The effect of these additions is to produce an actual picture of the miracle.

No. 113. From Tybroughney Cross. (9 in. × 7½ in.)
This and the following symbols are taken from the *Physiologus* or *Bestiary.*[17] The stag is there stated to have a great antipathy to serpents and to trample them to death whenever possible. It was therefore held to be an emblem of Christ triumphing over the Evil One, or of the Christian contending with the world.

No. 114. From Drumcliff Cross. (10 in. × 10 in.)
A cat-like animal with curiously humped back, which is carved in very high relief on the shaft, in a position corresponding to the lion-like animal on the other side.

The particular animal intended is doubtful, but it may be the *Panther* which took an important place in the Bestiary as an emblem of Christ. It was said to be loved and respected by all the other beasts except the *Dragon* which hated and wished to injure it, though unable to do so. The latter thus symbolised the Devil.

[17] Mr. Romilly Allen, *Early Christian Symbolism of Great Britain and Ireland,* pp. 334-341.

No. 115. From Tybroughney Cross. (16½ in. × 12 in.)

·This is the only carving yet found in Ireland of a Centaur with two axes; a form well known in Scotland.[18]   The other centaurs carved on Irish monuments hold bows and arrows or branches. (Compare No. 120.) The centaur, in these cases a compound of man and ass, being partly human and partly bestial, was looked upon as a symbol of the antagonism between good and evil in general, or of the deceitful man who appears to be good but is really evil.

Mr. Romilly Allen has included the centaur with two axes amongst the Pictish symbols; but the fact that it is thus found outside Scotland, and that even in Scotland it is not found on the earlier unshaped monuments, appear to indicate that it should rather be placed with the symbolic animals of the Bestiary which are carved on the same monuments.

No. 116. From Tybroughney Cross. (7½ in. × 7 in.)

The lion, which owing to the story related in the Bestiary, was regarded as a symbol of the resurrection. The fable is that the lion cubs remain without life for three days from birth, after which the old lion comes and breathes on them, thus awakening them.

No. 117. From a Cross at Inis Cealtra. (12 in. × 9 in.)

A symbolic animal of doubtful species, probably a hyena. This animal was thought to entice men to its den by imitating the human voice, and to devour them there: it was therefore used as an emblem of the Devil. The object in its mouth is a human leg, often used by the old designers to denote a carniverous animal, just as a branch marked a vegetable feeder. The panel is on the *sinister* side of the cross base; the dexter side is unfortunately broken away, but probably bore a symbol the meaning of which contrasted strongly with this one.

No. 118. From the North Cross, Duleek. (7 in. × 6 in.)

A panel containing a griffon. It is carved on the end of one arm of the cross; No. 122 occupies the corresponding panel on the other.   The griffon was said to live in deserts and to carry thither large animals as its prey; it therefore denoted the Devil carrying sinners to Hell. It is usually represented as having the head and wings of a bird, and the body and legs of a quadruped.

These characteristics can be recognised in the present carving, which is also interesting as showing the spiral at the junction of the wing and body and for the way in which the tail is bent in order that no part of the panel may remain unfilled.   A design almost identical with this forms part of the decoration of the western or tallest cross at Monasterboice.

No. 119. From Tybroughney Cross. (10 in. × 8½ in.)

A human-headed animal, apparently the *manticora* or man eater fabled to have the head of a man and the body of lion, and to feed on human

---

[18] Illustrated in *Early Christian Monuments of Scotland,* part iii., pp. 222 and 298. Also in *Early Christian Symbolism of Great Britain and Ireland,* p. 367.

flesh. It is thought to have originated from exaggerated accounts of the tiger,[19] and was often carved on monuments as an emblem of death.

This is almost the only Irish example known;[20] Scottish examples are illustrated in *Early Christian Monuments of Scotland* and *Early Christian Symbolism*. In one case the manticora is shown in the act of pursuing a man.

No. 120. From the Market Cross, Kells. (41 in. × 12½ in.)

A long panel containing two centaurs, one drawing a bow and the other holding out a branch. On the back of the former is a bird and above the latter a small animal.. There are also two eagles, one holding a fish and the other a lamb. The meaning of this has not been clearly made out, but the eagle and fish is known on Scottish stones as well as in manuscripts,[21] and may represent the sea as the centaur is used to typify the desert.

The Bestiary states that the eagle seizing the fish represents Christ taking possession of the souls of men. The centaur with the bow appears in the Bestiary under the name of Sagittarius, and the centaur with the branch is a well known classical design.

PLATES XLI. AND XLII. (PART OF).

No. 121. From Durrow Abbey Cross. (9½ in. × 7 in.)

A palm tree between two winged lions. The stone is greatly injured, but it is clear that each lion grasps the tree with one paw and that their heads are turned full face. This is an interesting example of one of the oldest and most widely spread of symbolic designs,[22] but it is difficult to say how it came to be carved on an Irish Christian monument. It is found on Assyrian slabs and cylinders, and on certain ancient buildings in Asia Minor. Variations of the design have men worshipping instead of animals, and a pillar or altar instead of a tree. The celebrated carving over the lion gate of Mycenae is of the latter form. Figure 14 shows Assyrian, Mycenaean, and Ionian examples for comparison.

No. 122. From the North Cross, Duleek. (7 in. × 6 in.)

A winged lion holding what appears to be a pole or staff. The meaning of this design and of its counterpart on the West Cross at Monasterboice might escape recognition, but on comparison with No. 121 it becomes evident that they are incomplete or abbreviated copies of the same subject. In the same way a small gem found in Crete shows a wild goat beside a tree, the second goat seen on larger specimens being omitted to save space.[23]

---

[19] Valentine Ball, *Proceedings of the Royal Irish Academy*, vol. xvi. (1884), p. 310.

[20] A small example from the doorway of Killeshin Church is illustrated in the *Journal of the Royal Society of Antiquaries of Ireland*, vol. xlviii. (1918), p. 183.

[21] A good example from St. Gall is shown in the *Ulster Journal of Archaeology*, vol. viii. (1860), plate IV., p. 304.

[22] See *Encyclopaedia Britannica* (11th ed.), vol, 19, p. 16, note.

[23] Illustrated in the *Journal of Hellenic Studies*, vol. xxi., p. 154.

In this design the lion has his tail raised, and he grasps the tree with both fore paws. The curve of the tail passes out over the moulding of the panel, which is unusual. '

No. 123. From the North Cross, Castledermot. (22 in. × 17 in.)

A curious figure crouched together and bound with cords or bandages. The head is shaped like that of an animal, and has a long tail or crest attached. This figure has been thought to represent a pagan interment, and thus to symbolise death.[24]

---

[24] Miss M. Stokes, *High Crosses of Castledermot and Durrow*, p. 2.

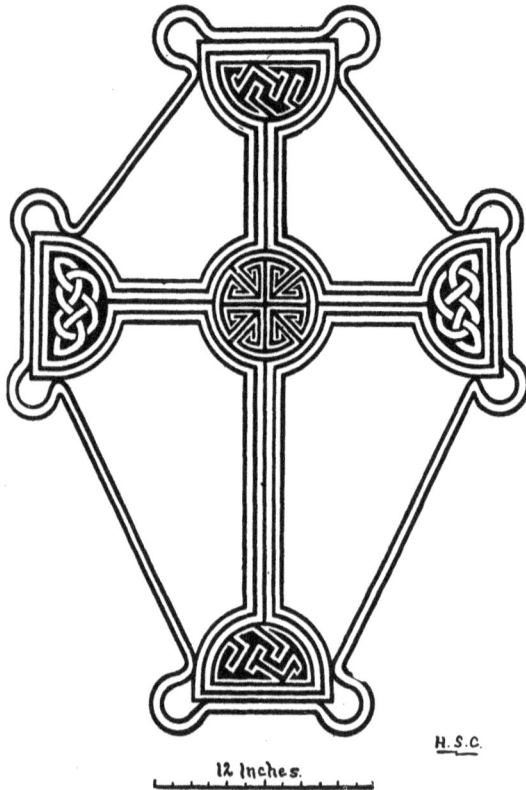

H.S.C.

12 Inches.

DESIGN RESTORED FROM A BROKEN CROSS-SLAB AT FUERTY. (1/10.)

CHAPTER X.

PICTORIAL DESIGNS

ASSING on to the pictorial panels carved in such numbers on the High Crosses, we find that they represent scenes and figures either religious and scriptural or local and historical in character. They are often in very high relief, but the figures are usually thickset and clumsy; a great contrast to the excellence of the linear and Zoömorphic designs. The early sculptors could, however, on occasion infuse no small share of vigour and action into their work, as may be seen for example, in Nos. 152, 154 and 155.

Many of the figures are of great interest as contemporary representations of dress, ornaments, and weapons. At Monasterboice, Clonmacnois, Durrow, Kells, Ahenny, and other places there are panels which preserve to us the costume of clerics, chiefs, and soldiers; and the forms of bells, crosiers, swords, spears, and shields; as well as the penanular brooch and the manner of wearing it, with other information.

The scripture and religious scenes include such subjects as the following, a few of the identifications being more or less uncertain:—

The Fall	Drumcliff, Monasterboice, &c.
Adam naming the animals	Ahenny.
Cain and Abel	Monasterboice, Kells, &c.
Noah driving animals	Kells, Castledermot, &c.
Noah in the Ark	Kells, Killary.
Sacrifice of Isaac	Durrow, Moone, &c.
Moses receiving the Law	Kells.
The hands of Moses held up	Monasterboice.
Moses striking the rock	Clonmacnois.
Sampson and the lion	Old Kilcullen.
David with lion and lamb	Old Kilcullen.
David and Goliath	Monasterboice.
David playing harp	Castledermot, Ullard.
Jonah cast into the Sea	Monasterboice.
Three children in furnace	Moone, Kells, &c.
Daniel in lions' den	Moone, Kells, &c.
Virgin and Child	Drumcliff, Killary.
Presentation in Temple	Durrow.
Baptism of Christ	Kells, Killary.

The Magi . . .	Monasterboice.
Flight into Egypt . .	Moone, Old Kilcullen.
Blessing of loaves and fishes .	Castledermot.
Twelve Apostles . .	Castledermot, Moone,
Christ seized by the Jews	Durrow, Clonmacnois.
Crucifixion . . .	Monasterboice, Durrow, &c.
Soldiers at the tomb . .	Durrow, Clonmacnois.
Last Judgment . .	Monasterboice.
Christ in glory . . .	Durrow, Monasterboice, &c.
Death of St. Peter . .	Kells, Castledermot.
Paul and Anthony breaking bread in the desert .	⎰Monasterboice. ⎱Kells, Castledermot, Moone.

The secular scenes represent persons fighting, hunting, travelling, playing musical instruments and going through various ceremonies, the meaning of which is often doubtful.

PLATES XLI. AND XLII.—(Continued).

No. 124. From Drumcliff Cross. (37 in. × 11 in.)

The Fall, one of the most frequently repeated of Scripture scenes. The foliage of the apple tree is here more elaborate than usual, and is treated in the same way as that of the flowering sceptre in the Last Judgment scenes. The tree has two stems round which the serpent is twisted, and below is a square of circular knotwork into which the roots are worked. The figures of Adam and Eve are placed facing the spectator, not in profile as in most cases; for instance the following:—

No. 125. From Muiredach's Cross, Monasterboice. (21 in. × 7 in.)

Figures of Adam and Eve with the tree, and of Cain and Abel. The tree is much simpler in form than in the last example, being no more than a trunk supporting two drooping branches covered with fruit. These branches form arches over the heads of the figures, and the latter are partially turned away though not quite in profile.

Cain is represented as striking Abel with a club or cleaver; the scene has sometimes been described as the expulsion from Eden, but the weapon and the act of striking the head do not seem appropriate to this. Both figures are alike, dressed in short tunics or kilts with ornamented borders.

No. 126. From the North Cross, Ahenny. (45 in. × 17 in.)

This panel occupies one side of the base and contains a man, a palm tree, and a number of animals. This and the palm trees mentioned in connection with Nos. 121 and 122 are the only instances of a tree, other than the vine and apple, being carved on this class of monument. The man stands under the palm and appears to watch rather than to hunt the animals; the subject may therefore be Adam naming the beasts. It may be mentioned, as having a bearing on this identification, that the palm tree used as an accessory often indicates that the scene represents Paradise.[1]

---

[1] Mentioned in the *Guide to the Early Christian and Byzantine Antiquities in the British Museum*, p. 18.

The animals can hardly be recognised with certainty, but two fighting or playing together are probably lions; there is also a stag or elk at the right hand end, while others resemble foxes and wolves. In the centre are two birds holding up an oval object and below them a two-toed animal of prehistoric aspect.

The subject of Adam amongst the animals is not unknown in early Christian art; it appears for instance on an ivory diptych of the fifth century now at Florence.[2]

No. 127. From the Market Cross, Kells. (46 in. × 12½ in.)

The subject here is a man holding a staff, and driving before him a number of animals of different kinds, including a boar and two stags. It is repeated on the South Cross, as well as on one of those at Castledermot, Co. Kildare.

The meaning of the design is uncertain; it differs from the ordinary hunting scenes in the number of different animals crowded together, and has been thought to represent Noah driving the animals into the Ark.

PLATES XLIII. AND XLIV.

No. 128. From the West Cross, Killary. (11 in. × 9 in.)

A representation of the Ark. It is shown as a small vessel with high curved ends, in the centre of which is a mast with yard and sail; the dove is perched on the top and holds a leaf. The heads of two occupants are seen and appear to fill the entire vessel. Below are three points, either mountain peaks or waves, probably the latter.

The Ark also appears on the West Cross at Kells, and is there made deeper and furnished with square windows in which heads are seen.[3] A head also appears above the deck, and feet in a corresponding position below the keel, so that the sculptor must have intended to show Noah in the act of leaving the Ark. Another carving of the Ark may be seen on a broken cross at Armagh.

No. 129. From the Market Cross, Kells. (12½ in. × 9½ in.)

This design probably represents Moses receiving the tables of the law. The Divine Hand has three fingers extended as in the act of benediction. At the base are two small figures which may be intended for the companions of Moses awaiting his return. The scene of Moses receiving the Law is found on sculptured sarcophagi at Rome.

No. 130. From Durrow Abbey Cross. (11 in. × 9 in.)

The Sacrifice of Isaac. Abraham stands with a sword in his hand, and grasps his son by the hair. Isaac, with an axe in his hand, kneels in front of an altar shaped like a stool; the bundle of faggots is bound on his back. In the background a figure holds a ram by the legs. This subject is a favourite one as a type of the Crucifixion; it is well seen on crosses at Moone Abbey, Kells, and Monasterboice.

---

[2] Illustrated in Lowrie's *Monuments of the Early Church*, p. 284.

[3] Illustrated in *Early Christian Symbolism of Great Britain and Ireland*, p. 232.

No. 131. From the West Cross, Old Kilcullen. (17½ in × 13 in.)

David rescuing the lamb from the lion. Sampson and the lion are often shown in the same way; both subjects are carved on this cross, but the presence of the lamb serves to distinguish between them.

No. 132. From the West Cross, Monasterboice. (15½ in. × 10½ in.)

Jonah cast out of the ship. The vessel is a boat built of curved planks and rowed with oars which pass through openings in the gunwale; the steering oar is also shown. The prophet is in the water and holds up his hands in supplication.

This design and the next were used as types of the descent into Hell. The subject has also been described as Peter walking on the water, but as there is only one figure outside of the boat it is more likely to represent Jonah.

No. 133. From the West Cross, Monasterboice. (16½ in. × 13¼ in.)

The three children in the furnace. They are shown kneeling, while an angel spreads his wings over them. At either side is a man lifting a faggot on a fork and holding an object like a horn in his mouth.

In the representation of the same subject at Moone Abbey the three are placed under an arch which presumably indicates the cover of the furnace: on this arch stands an angel with four wings. A third example, which more closely resembles the present one, is carved on the South Cross at Kells.

No. 134. From Moone Abbey Cross. (32 in. × 25 in.)

Daniel in the lions' den. This panel shows the typical number of lions, four at one side and three at the other. The number is, however, sometimes varied, probably for reasons of symmetry; at Castledermot and Kells there are four. In this instance the lions resemble swine as much as any other animals, and their tails hang down instead of being turned over their backs as is usual; at least in symbolic lions from the Bestiary.

No. 135. From Durrow Abbey Cross. (13½ in. × 7 in.)

This may represent the Holy Family. A suggestion has been made that it is the Flight into Egypt, but in that scene the ass is generally shown (though not warranted by Scripture), for which see No. 137. The plaiting of the hair and the ornamental borders of the robes are well seen.

No. 136. From Drumcliff Cross. (21 in. × 10 in.)

The Presentation in the Temple. These figures are rather worn, but enough remains to make the subject clear. At the sides of the panel are the rows of pellets which, in that position, are almost peculiar to Drumcliff Cross.

No. 137. From Moone Abbey Cross. (25 in. × 16½ in.)

The Flight into Egypt. The figures are curiously rude and thickset like all those at Moone, but they are in good preservation and there is no uncertainty as to the subject. This scene is also carved on the West Cross at Old Kilcullen, in the same district.

No. 138. From the West Cross, Kells. (20½ in. × 14 in.)

The Baptism of Christ. This carving is in good preservation and shows the dress of the time; also the supposed two sources of the Jordan. The Dove is represented descending in the centre, and the Baptist is pouring the water from a ladle.

This subject is pictured on the West Cross at Monasterboice, but is there almost torn away. Another example from the same district is shown in No. 139.

PLATES XLV. AND XLVI.

No. 139. From the West Cross, Killary. (12½ in. × 10 in.)

Another carved panel of the Baptism. This also shows the water poured from a spoon or ladle, and indicates the two sources of the river. A characteristic feature is that the streams of water are interlaced between the legs of the figures. The same scene is carved on a broken shaft in Armagh Cathedral. In a similar way, on the shrine of St. Moedoc in the National Museum, the feet of some of the figures are bound by an interlaced pattern of cords.

No. 140. From Moone Abbey Cross. (42 in. × 31 in.)

The Apostles. The figures are as short and square as all the others on this cross; they are placed in three rows, and no attempt is made to differentiate them.

No. 141. From Durrow Abbey Cross. (14 in. × 12½ in.)

A panel representing Christ seized by the Jews; it does not present any remarkable features, but gives some indication of dress.

No. 142. From the West Cross, Monasterboice. (30½ in. × 30¼ in.)

This is a typical Celtic representation of the Crucifixion, which differs from later designs in having the arms lowered instead of raised, the body erect, and apparently secured by cords as well as nails.[4] The head, though usually erect, is in this instance inclined. At either side are the sponge and spear bearers, and beside them are detached heads perhaps intended for those of spectators. Miss Margaret Stokes thought that such heads might symbolise the sun and moon, figures of which are found on some continental representations of the Crucifixion.

This scene appears on early crosses more frequently than any other; it is carved on at least forty monuments in Ireland. It has been remarked, however, that these monuments are not treated as the instrument of death in any realistic fashion; the Crucifixion being merely carved in a panel as other scenes are.[5] In some cases, as at Moone Abbey, Kells (South Cross) and Clonmacnois (South Cross), it is not even placed in one of the central panels. Other Crucifixions are illustrated in Plates IV., V., VII., VIII., XII.

---

[4] See Archdeacon Healy in the *Journal of the Royal Society of Antiquaries of Ireland,* vol. xxi. (1891), p. 452.

[5] See last reference.

No. 143.   From "Cross of the Scriptures," Clonmacnois.   (17 in. × 12 in.)

The soldiers at the tomb of Christ.   They are armed with spears, wear pointed helmets, and are shown with their heads nodding together.

The body is lying in an ordinary grave covered by a stone slab on which the soldiers sit.   The face is uncovered, or more probably covered by a separate cloth, and the body wrapped in bandages marked with three Greek crosses.[6]   At the head there seems to be an opening into the grave, and in this one of the watchers has placed his foot.   There is a very similar carving of this scene on Durrow Cross, and others at Monasterboice and Kells.

No. 144.   From the West Cross, Monasterboice.   (27 in. × 26 in.)

This panel is from the opposite side of the same cross as No. 142, and seems to show Christ coming in glory, standing on clouds, armed and surrounded by armed followers.   In one hand he holds both shield and sword and in the other what appears to be a club; his attendants also carry circular shields and short swords.

On most crosses the Judgment is shown instead, in which Christ holds the cross and flowering sceptre; of this No. 145 is a good example.

No. 145.   From Muiredach's Cross, Monasterboice.   (79 in. × 42½ in.)

The Last Judgment.   In the centre Christ stands holding cross and sceptre, over his head is a bird, probably the phoenix, as emblem of the Resurrection, and on either hand musicians with harp and pipe.   On the right hand are the blessed singing and playing; on the left the accursed are driven away by a devil armed with a trident.   Below is depicted St. Michael weighing souls and driving his spear into the mouth of a prostrate demon who is trying to upset the balance; above are three angels who probably hold the book of record.

PLATES XLVII. AND XLVIII.

No. 146.   From "Cross of the Scriptures," Clonmacnois.   (17 in. × 13½ in.)

A warrior and a cleric setting up a staff or post.   The details of dress are of much interest; the ecclesiastic wears a long robe, the hem of which is decorated by a row of pellets, and over this a short cloak provided with a hood.   The chief or warrior is dressed in a short belted tunic, and has a sword suspended from a shoulder belt.

The round object above the staff is seen on close examination to be a human head, but owing to the worn condition of the stone it is not clear whether the head is carved on the staff or belongs to a spectator in the background; the latter is probable.   It has been suggested that this panel may represent Dermot Mac Cearbhaill helping St. Ciaran to erect the posts of his church, as described in the *Annals of Clonmacnois*.[7]

No. 147.   From Dysert O'Dea Cross.   (29 in. × 21 in.)

A panel containing four men, or possibly five, as one end is broken The central pair are engaged in setting up a tau-cross or crosier, the height

---

[6] Perhaps seals.

[7] P. 79. A.D. 547. Sée also T. J. Westropp in the *Journal of the Royal Society of Antiquaries of Ireland*, vol. xxxvii. (1907), p. 293.

of which is about equal to their own. One of the outer figures holds a crosier of the usual shape, and the other may have done so when complete.

This scene probably commemorates the fixing of a boundary mark like the cross of similar form which still exists at Kilnaboy in the same district. Tau crosiers are represented on other monuments as held in the hands of clerics, and an actual specimen may be examined in the National Museum.

No. 148. From the North Cross, Ahenny. (45 in. × 15 in.)

This is one side of the base, and is carved with seven large figures of ecclesiastics. The central figure shows the full face, those at the sides being in profile and holding crosiers in their hands. All are dressed in long robes covered by shorter ones, and behind each head an object, no doubt a hood of some kind, stands up stiffly. The scene may represent a procession in which the figures shown in profile really walked two and two behind their superior.

This carving illustrates well the early Irish form of crosier, which is entirely distinct from the spirally curved type used in other countries. These crosiers were simply the walking staves used by the founders of churches, enshrined in decorated cases and carried by the successors of the founders as emblems of their authority.

No. 149. From the West Cross, Old Kilcullen. (14 in. × 13 in.)

This remarkable carving seems to represent an ecclesiastical ceremony of some kind. An erect figure holds an axe in one hand and a crosier in the other; the foot of this crosier is placed on the body of a man lying prostrate and bound. A bell of early type and a square object—intended most likely for a *cumdach* or book shrine—fill the remaining portions of the panel. Miss Margaret Stokes identifies the principal figure as the first bishop of Kilcullen, he having been nicknamed *Mac Táil*, or Son of the Axe, because his father was a wright or carpenter.[8]

Similar scenes are carved on other crosses; for instance, at Kells and Monasterboice two ecclesiastics are shown placing their crosiers on the body of a man in a reversed position. At Clonmacnois a seated figure holds a book and presses an owl-headed staff on the head of a prostrate body. This has been explained as the triumph of Learning over Ignorance.

No. 150. From the North Cross, Ahenny. (38 in. × 15 in.)

One of the most striking designs on any Irish monument, but of doubtful meaning. A headless body is tied on an ass which is led by a man holding a crosier, and preceded by two others, one of whom bears a ringed cross. A dog walks beside the ass, and the rear is brought up by a man carrying a small figure, perhaps a child, on his back; two birds perch on the body and tear the flesh. The man leading the ass has a rounded object slung behind him, which is almost certainly the head belonging to the dead body.

The scene is evidently a funeral procession of some kind, but the difficulty is that if it represents the burial of a friend the birds would not be allowed to attack the body, and if that of an enemy so much ceremony,

---

[8] *High Crosses of Castledermot and Durrow*, p. 4.

including the carrying of a cross, would hardly be resorted to. This scene is repeated on the cross at Dromiskin, in Co. Louth. See note in preface.

No 151.   From Muiredach's Cross, Monasterboice.   (20 in. × 19½ in.)

Three figures in high relief representing an ecclesiastic attacked by robbers. It might be taken for the seizure of Christ by the Jews, but that the same robbers appear in the panels above dressed in ecclesiastical costume (but still retaining their moustaches) and receiving instruction and a blessing.[9]

The details of dress are very clear and interesting; the central figure wears a long robe covered by a shorter one secured by a penanular brooch on the right shoulder. The robbers are dressed in closely-fitting garments which leave the arms and legs bare; they are armed with swords, and have moustaches, but not beards.

No. 152.   From the Market Cross, Kells.   (41 in. × 12 in.)

An actual combat between two men armed with spears and three with clubs or axes; all five have circular shields which recall those of wood and leather in the collection of the Royal Irish Academy. The shields carried by the spear-men are shown edgeways and have projecting points; they seem to be bent back as if made of a flexible material like leather.

The other shields face the spectator and are round and flat, any central projection they may have had being worn away. Central bosses are generally shown on shields, and it is probable that they originally existed in this instance. All the figures have one knee on the ground, which may have been their way of fighting, or merely a device of the sculptor to make them fit the available space.

No. 153.   From the South Cross, Ahenny.   (16 in. × 14 in.)

This is the least injured of the eight panels on the base, all of which seemed to have contained hunting scenes. It shows a horseman, two dogs and two large and clumsy animals which are probably intended for bears; they have, it is true, short curly tails, but this may be due to want of knowledge on the sculptor's part. The hunter is riding along followed by the smaller of the two dogs, while in the background the bears are attacking the larger dog. This design is a good example of the placing of spirals on the bodies of animals.

PLATES XLIX. and L.

No. 154.   From the Market Cross, Kells.   (48 in. × 12 in.)

Four horsemen in single file. The stone is greatly injured, but it can still be seen that the riders carry swords and circular shields. The foremost seems to have horns or wings attached to his helmet, but this is uncertain.

No. 155.   From the North Cross, Ahenny.   (38 in. × 15 in.)

, Two horsemen and a chariot from the base of the cross. The horsemen come first and are accompanied by an animal of rather curious form,

---

[9] See Plate iv., where all three scenes are shown.

presumably a hound. The chariot contains two men, and is drawn by two horses harnessed by straps round their chests. Above the horses is a doubtful object occupying the place where the reins should be, but much too wide for them unless, perhaps, the cutting of this part has not been finished. At the top of the panel is a small dog which looks as near as the chariot, though intended to be in the background. This is one of the most life-like designs found on any monument of the period.

No. 156. From Bealin Cross. (20 in. × 8½ in.)

A hunting scene of considerable interest; it is arranged in an upright form to suit its position on the shaft. At the base is a horseman armed with a spear, and above a spirited representation of a stag at bay, its leg held by a large dog whose shape suggests that of the Irish wolf-hound. An otherwise vacant space behind the hunter is filled by a triquetra. The rough surface and coarse grain of the stone make the design less effective than it should be. There is a similar scene on the Market Cross at Kells; in it a man on foot is seen in the act of spearing a stag, while a hound springs on its back. Another example is carved on a broken shaft, now in Temple Dowling, at Clonmacnois; but there the hunter and the stag are in separate panels, and the latter is caught by the foot in a trap which suggests one of the objects known as "otter traps."[10]

No. 157. From "Cross of the Scriptures," Clonmacnois. (17 in. × 8 in.)

A musician dressed in a long robe, and playing a kind of mouth organ with several pipes of different lengths. Beside him is an extraordinary figure which the late Mr. T. J. Westropp compared to the *bagpipe-devils* of medieval manuscripts.[11] In front of the piper are two cats with tails and legs interlaced. The cat rarely appears in early sculpture; as an instance, those on Muiredach's Cross may be mentioned. It has been suggested that in this case the animals indicate a joke on the part of the sculptor who wished to give posterity a hint of what the pipes sounded like.

No. 158. From the South Cross, Castledermot. (9½ in. × 8 in.)

A seated harper, illustrating an early form of harp and the method of playing it. The material of the carving is a rough granite, and the details are not well preserved, but the harp is clearly square with an arched top and six strings. It forms a strong contrast to the triangular harp seen elsewhere, for instance on the shrine of St. Moedoc. A harper is carved on the cross at Ullard, in Kilkenny, but is almost worn away.

No. 159. From the South Cross, Castledermot. (9 in. × 5 in.)

The rude figure of a chief or warrior bearing a large sword and a small shield or buckler; he wears a long garment, but owing to the roughness of the stone few details are apparent.

No. 160. From "Cross of the Scriptures," Clonmacnois. (16½ in. × 13 in.)

In this panel are two chiefs standing side by side, supporting some small object between them and also holding sheathed swords. They have long hair, moustaches and beards, the latter in one case plaited and in

---

[10] *Proceedings, Society of Antiquaries, Scotland,* vol. xxxi (1896-7), p. 310.
[11] *Journal, Royal Society of Antiquaries, Ireland,* vol. xxxvii (1907), p. 296.

the other curled outwards. Each wears a long robe secured by a belt and over it a short coat or cloak with a large brooch or cross on the right shoulder. Except that they carry swords their dress resembles that of the ecclesiastic in No. 146; this may, indeed, have been the dress worn by all persons of distinction in time of peace.

No. 161. From the West Cross, Monasterboice. (18 in. × 10 in.)

A seated figure holding a shield in the left hand and a large round object in the right; this may be a portion of food for which the dogs below and the bird on his shoulder are clamouring. The dogs are shown as jumping up with their backs to their master, a position which seems quite unnatural, but is repeated in the next panel. It may be due to some convention which is now forgotten.

No. 162. From Durrow Abbey Cross. (13¼ in. × 8 in.)

The same design as in No. 161 slightly modified and more carefully carved. In this instance the chief has thick curled hair, long moustaches and closely plaited beard. In his right hand he holds a sword, and in his left both spear and shield. Two dogs are shown at the sides as in the last example; perhaps they are placed in the upright position merely from want of space.[12] It is noteworthy that this and other figures of the same kind are shown *bare-headed*. Miss Margaret Stokes has represented this figure as wearing a crown,[13] but the original carving does not support this.

---

[12] These designs may have some connection with those in Nos. 100 and 101.
[13] *High Crosses of Castledermot and Durrow.*

DESIGN FROM A BROKEN SLAB FORMERLY AT CLONMACNOIS. (1/8.)

INDEX TO LOCALITIES

SHOWING THE DESIGNS TAKEN FROM EACH

Locality and County	Ordnance Map	Illustrations [1]
AHENNY, TIPPERARY	N.E. 79	Nos. 9, 14, 15, 34, 36, 57, 62, 69, 77, 92, 126, 148, 150, 153, 155. D, E. Fig. 2. A. Fig. 3. A. Fig. 4. A. Fig. 5. E, F. Fig. 7. D. Fig. 9. B. Fig. 11.
ARDANE, TIPPERARY	N.E. 74	Nos. 21, 42, 65. D. Fig. 7.
BEALIN, WESTMEATH	N.E. 29	Nos. 16, 38, 39, 67, 79, 91, 156. C. Fig. 6.
BOHO, FERMANAGH	N.W. 21	Nos. 2, 50.
CAHERLEHILLAN, KERRY	S.E. 70	J. Fig. 9.
CARNDONAGH, DONEGAL	S.W. 11	Nos. 23, 26, 51, 54.
CASTLEDERMOT, KILDARE	N.W. 40	Nos. 1, 12, 60, 123, 158, 159.
CHURCH ISD. (WATERVILLE), KERRY	N.W. 98	O. Fig. 9.
CLONBURREN, ROSCOMMON	N.E. 56	E. Fig. 4.
CLONCA, DONEGAL	N.W. 12	No. 33.
CLONE, WEXFORD	S.E. 15	No. 24.
CLONFERT, GALWAY	S.W. 101	C. Fig. 3. C, H. Fig. 8.
CLONMACNOIS KING'S CO.	S.E. 5	Nos. 20, 22, 66, 105, 110, 143, 146, 157, 160. Fig. 1. B, E. Fig. 3. A, D. Fig. 6. A, B, H. Fig. 7. F, G, I. Fig. 8. C, G, K, M, N. Fig. 9.
DONAGHMORE, TYRONE	S.W. 46	L. Fig. 9.
DROMISKIN, LOUTH	S.W. 12	C. Fig. 11.

[1] No. — refers to designs shown in the plates.
Fig. — refers to designs shown in the text.

Locality and County	Ordnance Map	Illustrations [1]
DRUMCLIFF, SLIGO	S.E. 8	Nos. 7, 8, 49, 86, 114, 124, 136.
DULEEK, MEATH	S.W. 27	Nos. 4, 43, 44, 80, 82, 84, 85, 106, 107, 111, 118, 122. G. Fig. 6.
DURROW ABBEY, KING'S CO.	S.W. 9	Nos. 10, 11, 98, 121, 130, 135, 141, 162. A. Fig. 2. F. Fig. 3.
DYSERT O'DEA, CLARE	N.W. 25	Nos. 31, 56, 59, 68, 72, 89, 90, 94, 99, 147. E. Fig. 10.
EMLAGH, ROSCOMMON	S.W. 27	No. 37.
FAHAN MURA, DONEGAL	N.W. 58	No. 55.
FERNS, WEXFORD	N.E. 15	No. 58.
FUERTY, ROSCOMMON	S.W. 39	No. 109. I. Fig. 6.
GALLEN PRIORY, KING'S CO.	S.E. 14	No. 41. C. Fig. 7.
GLENCAR (CLOON), KERRY	S.W. 82	D. Fig. 8. B, E. Fig. 9.
GLENCOLUMBKILLE, DONEGAL	S.E. 80	E. Fig. 8.
GLENDALOUGH, WICKLOW	N.E. 23	C, F. Fig. 4. I, P. Fig. 9. C. Fig. 12.
GRAIGUENAMANAGH, KILKENNY	N.E. 29	No. 13.
INCHAGOIL, GALWAY	N.E. 40	A. Fig. 8.
INISBOFINNE, WESTMEATH	N.W. 15	F. Fig. 9.
INIS CEALTRA, CLARE	N.E. 29	Nos. 25, 117. D. Fig. 4.
INISMURRAY, SLIGO	S.E. 1	A. Fig. 9.
KELLS, MEATH	N.W. 17	Nos. 19, 74, 78, 81, 93, 100, 104, 120, 127, 129, 138, 152, 154. E. Fig. 5. I. Fig. 7. B, F. Fig. 10.

[1] No. — refers to designs shown in the plates.
Fig. — refers to designs shown in the text.

Locality and County	Ordnance Map	Illustrations [1]
KILFENORA, CLARE	N.W. 16	Nos. 47, 48, 64. B. Fig. 8.
KILKIERAN, KILKENNY	S.E. 34	Nos. 29, 30, 32, 35. B. Fig. 4. B. Fig. 5.
KILLAMERY, KILKENNY	S.W. 30	Nos. 27, 61, 96. C. Fig. 2. H. Fig. 9.
KILLARY, MEATH	N.E. 12	Nos. 128, 139.
KILLEANY (ARAN), GALWAY	N.W. 119	No. 28.
KINNITTY, KING'S CO.	N.E. 36	Nos. 3, 40, 88. B. Fig. 2. G. Fig. 3. A. Fig. 12.
MONA INCHA, TIPPERARY	N.W. 18	B. Fig. 6.
MONASTERBOICE, LOUTH	N.W. 21	Nos. 17, 18, 52, 53, 63, 70, 75, 83, 95, 97, 103, 108, 125, 132, 133, 142, 144, 145, 151, 161. F. Fig. 2. H. Fig. 3. C, D, F, G. Fig. 5. G, J. Fig. 7. C, D. Fig. 10.
MOONE ABBEY, KILDARE.	S.W. 36	Nos. 101, 112, 134, 137, 140.
OLD KILCULLEN, KILDARE	S.E. 28	Nos. 131, 149. B. Fig. 12.
TERMONFECHIN, LOUTH	S.W. 22	Nos. 45, 73, 76. F. Fig. 6. A. Fig. 10.
TIHILLY, KING'S CO.	S.E. 8	Nos. 5, 6, 46, 71, 87, 102.
TULLYLEASE, CORK	N.W. 6	I. Fig. 3. E. Fig. 6.
TYBROUGHNEY, KILKENNY	S.E. 38	Nos. 113, 115, 116, 119. A. Fig. 11.
TYNAN ABBEY, ARMAGH	S.W. 11	D. Fig. 3. H. Fig. 6.

[1] No. — refers to designs shown in the plates.
Fig. — refers to designs shown in the text.

A Spiral Design adapted from
A and B, Fig. 11; No. 77, &c.

Plates

PLATE I.

The North Cross at Ahenny, Co. Tipperary.

PLATE II.

The South Cross at Ahenny, Co. Tipperary.

PLATE III.

The Cross at Durrow Abbey, County Offaly.

PLATE IV.

Muirdedach's Cross at Monasterboice, County Louth.

PLATE V.

The South Cross at Castledermot, County Kildare.

PLATE VI.

The Crosses at Arboe, County Tyrone, and at Moone Abbey,
County Kildare.

PLATE VII.

The East Cross at Drumcliff, County Sligo.

PLATE VIII.
The Cross at Dysert O'Dea, County Clare.

PLATE IX.
Erect Cross-slab at Fahan Mura, County Donegal.

PLATE X.

Erect Cross-slab at Carndonagh, County Donegal.

PLATE XI.
Erect Cross-slab at Reisk, County Kerry.

PLATE XII.

Erect Cross-slabs at Inishkea North, County Mayo (A), Caherlehillan, County Kerry (B), and Cliffony, County Sligo (C).

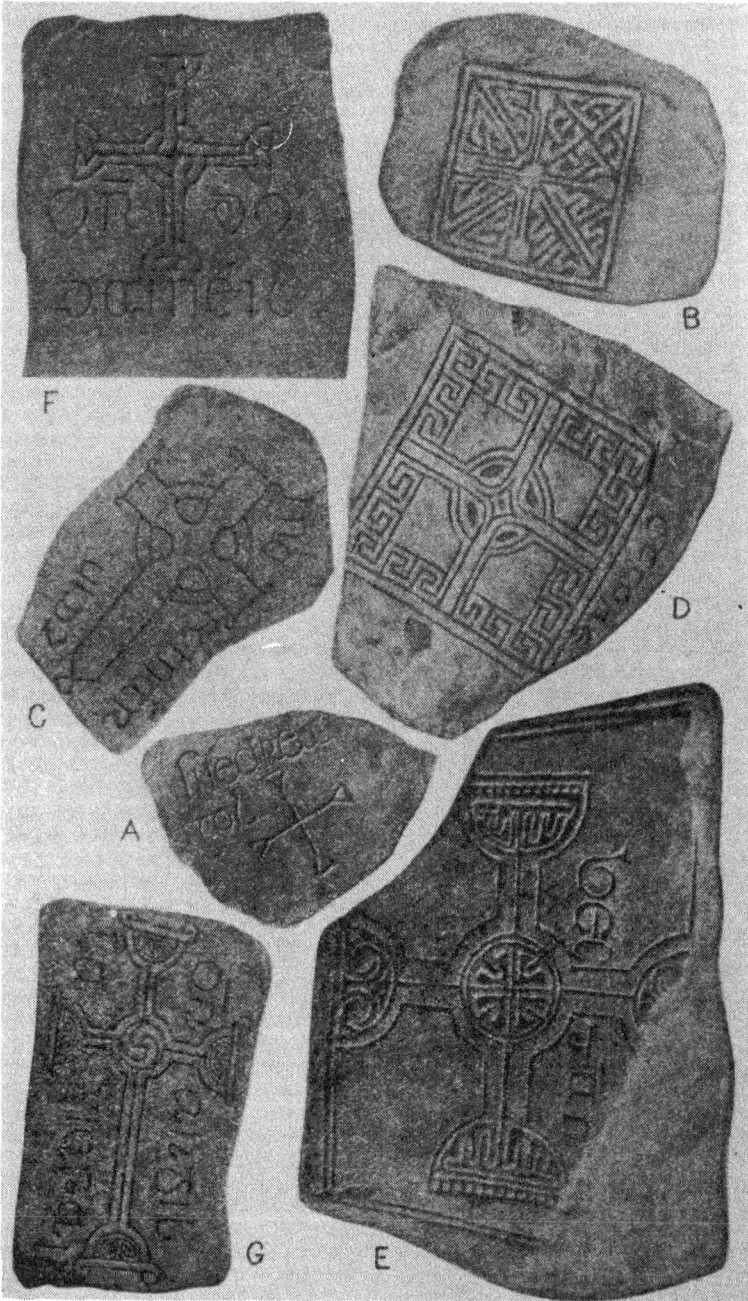

PLATE XIII.

Recumbent Slabs at Clonmacnois (A, D, F, G), Inis Cealtra (B), Inisbofinne (C), Clonfert (E).

PLATE XIV.

Recumbent Slabs at Tullylease (A), Durrow Abbey (B), and Clonmacnois (C).

PLATE XIVa.
Divergent Spiral or Trumpet Pattern, from the North Cross at Ahenny,
County Tipperary. (See also Plate I).

PLATE XV.
Spiral Patterns; Untouched.

PLATE XVI.
The Same Patterns; Restored.

PLATE XVII.

Spiral Patterns; Untouched.

PLATE XVIII.

The Same Patterns; Restored.

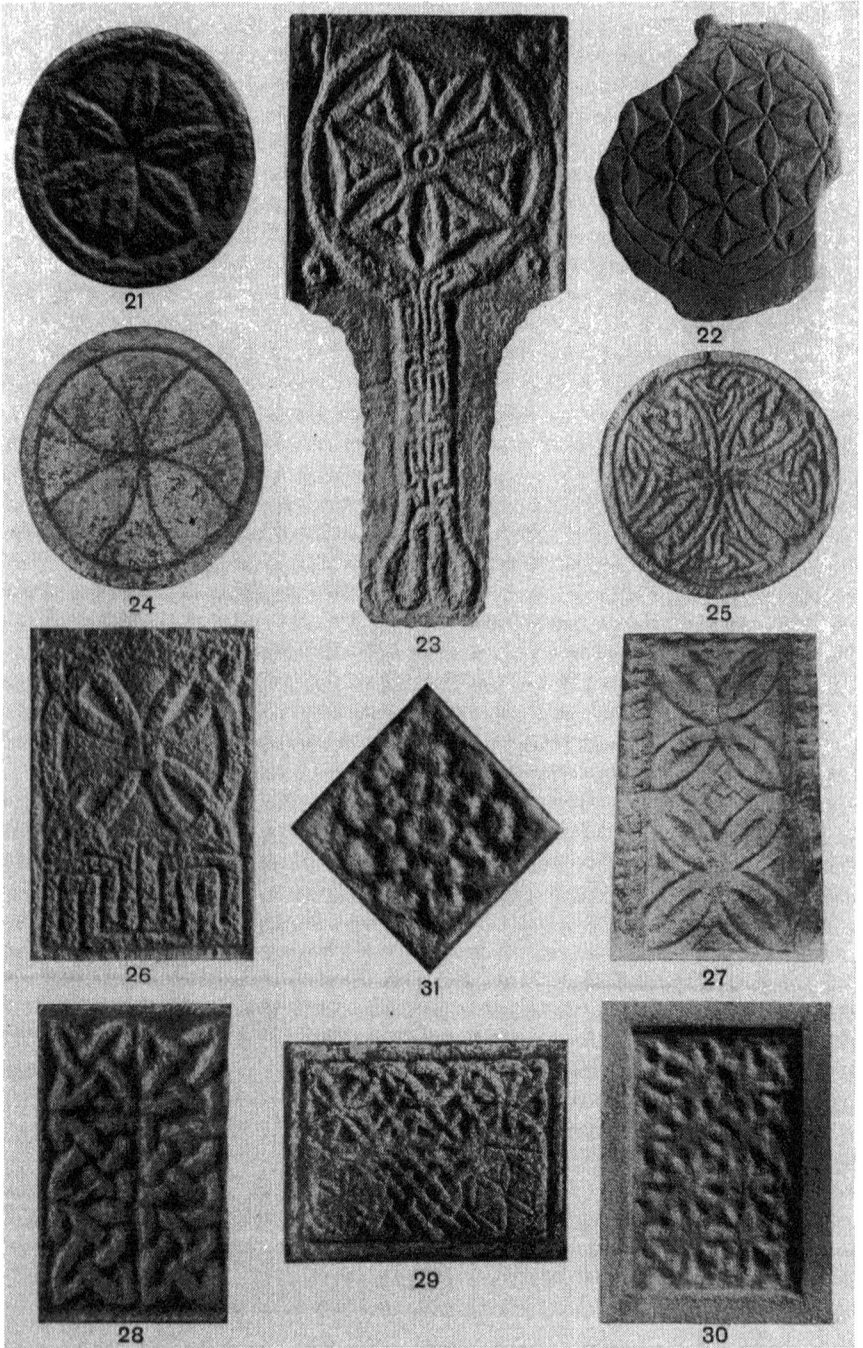

PLATE XIX.

Star Patterns; Untouched.

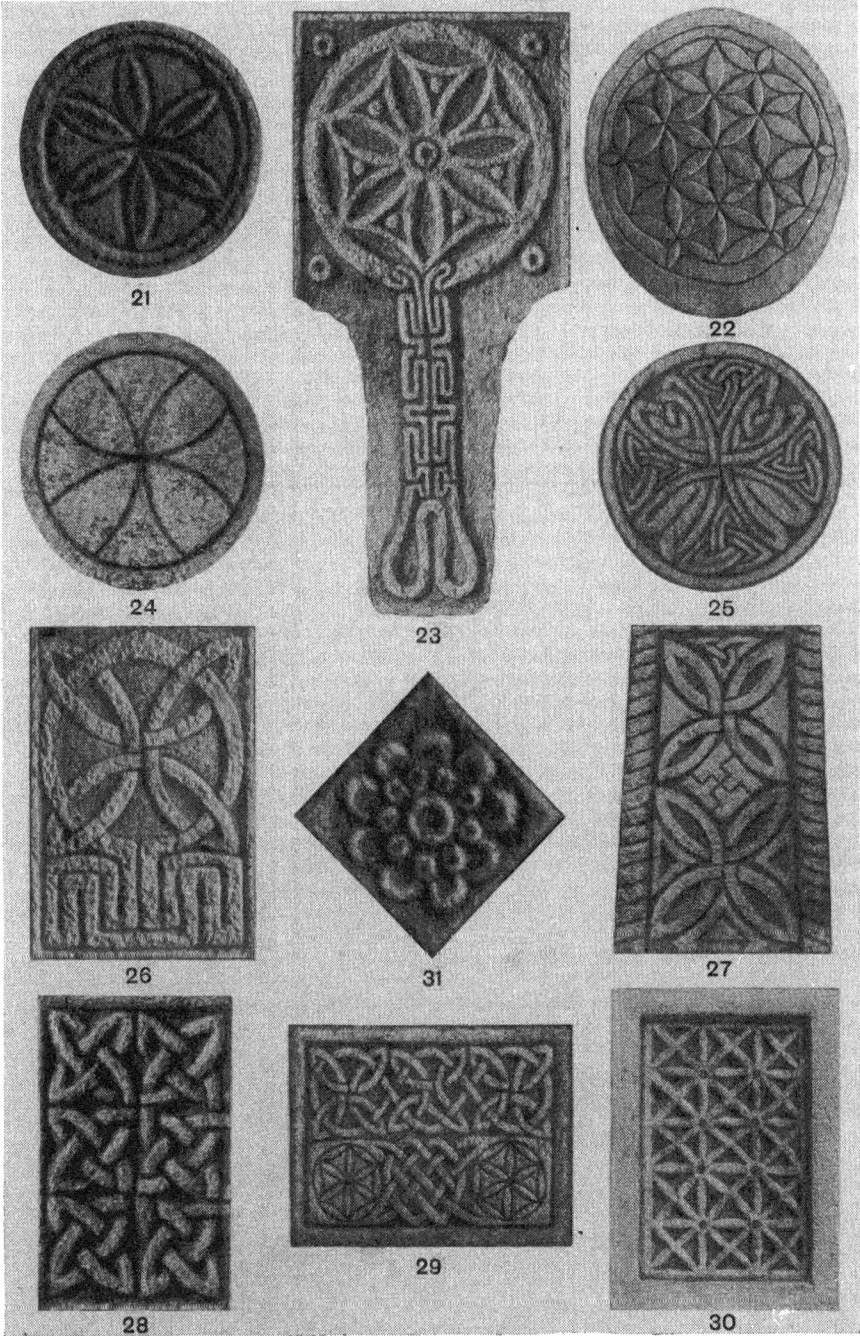

PLATE XX.

The Same Patterns; Restored.

PLATE XXI.

Interlaced Patterns; Untouched.

32   34   33

35   36   37

38   40   39

PLATE XXII.

The Same Patterns; Restored.

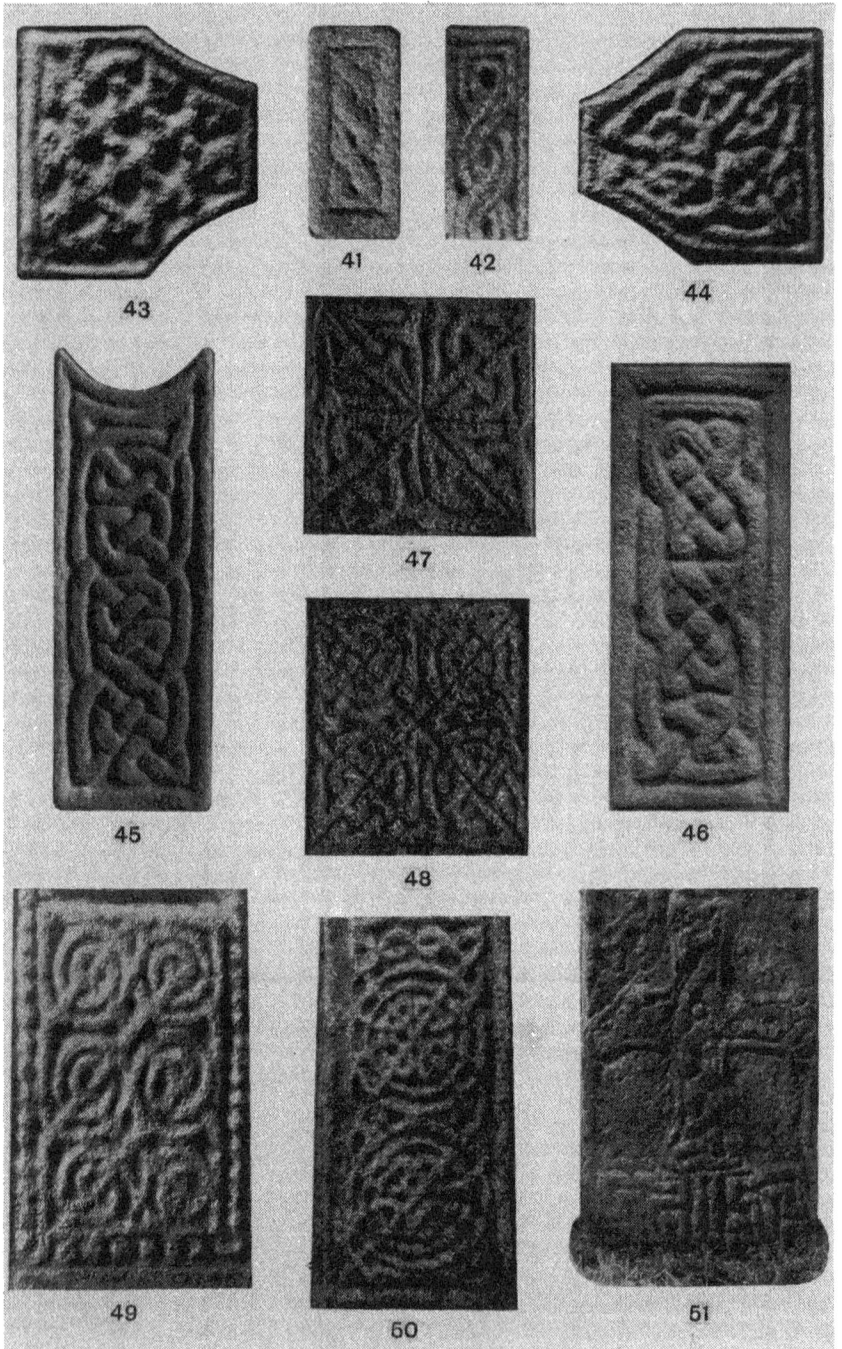

PLATE XXIII.

Interlaced Patterns; Untouched.

PLATE XXIV.

The Same Patterns; Restored.

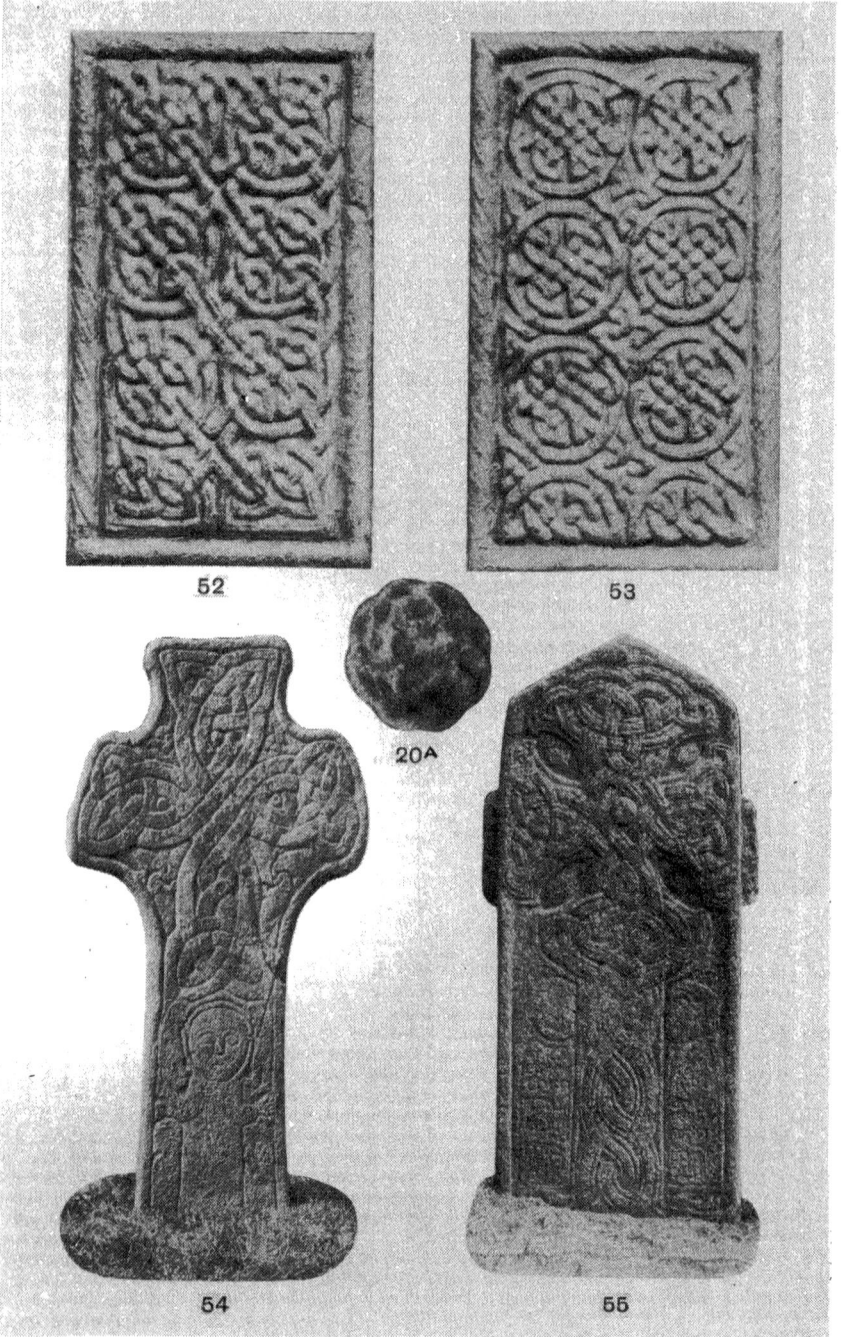

52 53

20A

54 55

PLATE XXV.
Interlaced Patterns; Untouched.

52 53

20^

54 55

PLATE XXVI.

The Same Patterns; Restored.

PLATE XXVII.
Fret Patterns; Untouched.

PLATE XXVIII.

The Same Patterns; Restored.

68

67

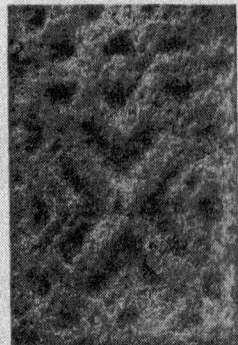

69

70

71

72

74

73

75

PLATE XXIX.

Fret Patterns; Untouched.

68

67

69

70

71

72

74

73

75

PLATE XXX.

The Same Patterns; Restored.

77   76   78

79   81   80

82   84   83

PLATE XXXI.

Zoomorphic Designs; Untouched.

77

76

78

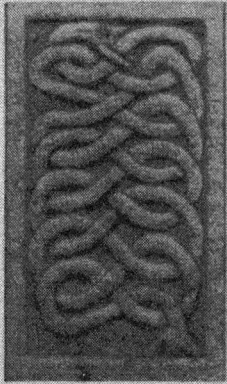

79

81

80

82

84

83

PLATE XXXII.

The Same Designs; Restored.

85

86

87

88

89

91

90

92

93

PLATE XXXIII.

Zoomorphic Designs; Untouched.

86

85

87

88

90

89

92

91

93

PLATE XXXIV.

The Same Designs; Restored.

94

95

97

98

96

PLATE XXXV.

Zoomorphic Designs; Untouched.

94

95

97

98

96

PLATE XXXVI.

The Same Designs; Restored.

PLATE XXXVII.
Symbolic Designs; Untouched.

99
100
101
102
104
105
103
106
107
109
108
110

PLATE XXXVIII.

The Same Designs; Restored.

PLATE XXXIX.
Symbolic Designs; Untouched.

111

112

113

114

115

116

117

118

119

120

PLATE XL.

The Same Designs; Restored.

123

121

122

125

124

126

127

PLATE XLI.

Symbolic and Pictorial Designs; Untouched.

123

121

122

125

124

126

127

PLATE XLII.

The Same Designs; Restored.

129

128

130

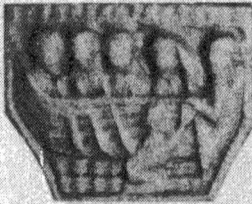

132

131

133

135

134

136

137

138

PLATE XLIII.

Pictorial Designs; Untouched.

129

128

130

132

131

133

135

134

136

137

138

PLATE XLIV.

The Same Designs; Restored.

139 140 141

142 143 144

145

PLATE XLV.
Pictorial Designs; Untouched.

139

140

141

142

143

144

145

PLATE XLVI.

The Same Designs; Restored.

146

147

148

149

151

150

152

153

PLATE XLVII.

Pictorial Designs; Untouched.

146

147

148

149

151

150

152

153

PLATE XLVIII.

The Same Designs; Restored.

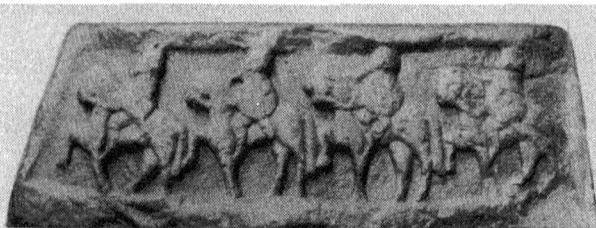

154

155

156

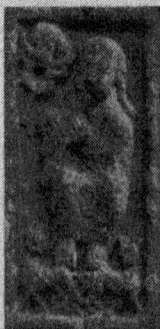

157

158

159

161

160

162

PLATE XLIX.

Pictorial Designs; Untouched.

154

155

156

157

158

159

161

160

162

PLATE L.

The Same Designs; Restored.

PLATE LI.

Interlaced Work, Broken Plait, from The North Cross at Ahenny, County
Tipperary.

www.ingramcontent.com/pod-product-compliance
Lightning Source LLC
Chambersburg PA
CBHW021405090426
42742CB00009B/1014